WHS

LITERATURE GUIDE

LITERATURE GUIDE

AS/A2

Othello

First published 2003
exclusively for WHSmith by
Hodder & Stoughton Educational
338 Euston Road
London
NW1 3BH

ISBN 0 340 87298 5

Impression number   10 9 8 7 6 5 4 3 2 1
                     2009 2008 2007 2006 2005 2004 2003

Copyright © 2003 Steve Eddy

All rights reserved. No part of this publication may be reproduced or transmitted in any form or by any means, electronic or mechanical, including photocopying, recording or any information storage and retrieval system, without permission in writing from the publisher or under licence from the Copyright Licensing Agency Limited. Further details of such licences (for reprographic reproduction) may be obtained from the Copyright Licensing Agency Limited, of 90 Tottenham Court Road, London W1P 9HE

Illustrations: Karen Donnelly

Typeset by Transet Limited, Leamington Spa, England.
Printed in Great Britain for Hodder & Stoughton Educational, a division of Hodder Headline Plc, 338 Euston Road, London NW1 3BH by Cox & Wyman Ltd., Reading, Berkshire.

Contents

Introduction: how to study	**vii**
●Studying Shakespeare at AS and A2 level	vii
●Enhance your learning power	vii
●How to use this guide	ix
Context	**1**
●Shakespeare's sources	1
●Genre	2
●Moors in London	4
●Venice and Cyprus	4
●Dating and texts	6
The story of *Othello* (Act by Act)	**7**
Characterization	**10**
●Othello: noble but credulous soldier	10
●Iago: malicious manipulator	13
●Desdemona: virtuous victim	17
●Cassio: open-hearted, chivalrous lieutenant	18
●Emilia: world-weary but well-meaning wife	18
●Bianca: maligned mistress	19
●Roderigo: duped gentleman	20
●Brabantio: outraged father	20
●Minor characters: Duke of Venice, Gratiano, Lodovico, Montano	21
Themes	**23**
●Love and sex	24
●Jealousy and envy	27
●Appearance and reality	29
●Race and otherness	31
●The individual and society	32
Language, style and structure	**34**
●Poetry and prose	34

• Shakespeare's imagery	36
• Dating by style	39
• Structure	39

Commentary — 44
- Act 1 — 44
- Act 2 — 52
- Act 3 — 59
- Act 4 — 68
- Act 5 — 74

Critical approaches — 87
- Reading critically — 87
- Early views — 88
- More recent views — 89

How to get an 'A' in English Literature — 95

The exam essay — 96

Model answers — 97
- Question 1 — 97
- Question 2 — 100

Taking it further — 104

Glossary of literary terms — 106

Index — 109

INTRODUCTION: HOW TO STUDY

Studying Shakespeare at AS and A2 level

Your study of Shakespeare at Key Stage 3 and at GCSE will form a good basis for your work at more advanced levels. However, you will now have to extend some of your existing skills. In particular, you will need to be more aware of the many possible critical approaches to the play, which is why this guide devotes a chapter to them. You will also need to be more aware of the context of the play in social, historical and literary terms, and so one chapter in this guide focuses on that. At the very least, you should be able to compare it with another Shakespeare play that you have studied, which will help to throw *Othello* into perspective.

The study of characters remains important, but you will be expected to have a deeper awareness of their dramatic role within the play. Themes remain important, but you will need to show more awareness of how they are reflected in the language of the play, and be able to demonstrate how Shakespeare's language achieves its effects. In doing this, you will need to make correct use of technical terms such as 'metaphor' and 'simile'.

Enhance your learning power

This guide is of course no substitute for careful reading of the text. You will probably read the play in class, but it will help if you read it to yourself as well. When you have read the text and understood the plot and the character relationships, you need to develop an overview of the play. Ideally you should be able to remember which Act any major event or speech occurs in, and perhaps even which scene, so that you can find it easily. This will help when looking for quotes or comparing scenes. The section in this guide entitled 'The story of *Othello*' will help you to achieve this.

OTHELLO

PREVIEW AND REVIEW

How you go about learning is important. A general principle is to get into a habit of *preview* and *review*. In other words, skim over what you are going to read – whether in the play or in this guide, read it, then review it. *Previewing* will help you to be in control of your study and to read in a purposeful way – a bit like climbing up a hill and 'getting the lie of the land' before setting off on a journey. *Reviewing* will help to fix what you have read in your mind. Repeat the review at intervals – perhaps a few hours later, then the next day, then a few days later, and you'll fix what you've learned in your memory for life. In this guide, the bullet point lists at the start of each scene in the Commentary will help you to preview the scene, and the questions at the ends of sections will help you to review what you have learned.

ACTIVE LEARNING

Try to read Shakespeare, and this guide, actively, not passively. Seek to have your questions answered as you read. When reading the play, consider how what you are reading could be interpreted, either critically or on stage. Be confident that your own interpretations are worth pursuing providing you can back them up with evidence from the text. Try to imagine scenes on stage, and try to visualize any imagery used: visualization is a great memory aid.

You will find that it helps to have your own copy of the play so that you can write notes on it. It may also help to write notes on this guide. Make all your notes as visual as possible and use the section at the back of this book. Use colour and headings. Use spider diagrams or other visual forms of idea-mapping.

Make use of people around you. Get friends and relatives to test you. You will also find that discussing the play, especially key issues such as Iago's motives, will help you to develop your own ideas and become increasingly clear about what happens in the play and how it can be interpreted.

INTRODUCTION

How to use this guide

This guide assumes that you have already read *Othello*, although you could read 'Context' and 'The story of *Othello*' first. It is best to use the guide alongside the play. You could read the 'Characterization' and 'Themes' sections without referring to the play, but you will get more out of these if you do refer to it.

THE SECTIONS

The 'Commentary' section can be used in a number of ways. One way is to read a scene, and then read the relevant commentary. Keep on until you come to a test section, test yourself – then have a break! Alternatively, read the Commentary for a scene, then read that scene in the play, then go back to the Commentary. See what works best for you.

'Critical approaches' sums up the main critical views and interpretations of the play. Your own response is important, but be aware of these approaches too. 'How to get an "A" in English Literature' gives valuable advice on what to look for in a text, and what skills you need to develop in order to achieve your personal best. 'The exam essay' is a useful 'night before' reminder of how to tackle exam questions, though it will help you more if you also look at it much earlier in the year. 'Model answers' gives examples of A-grade essays, including a textual analysis.

Line references are to the Arden Shakespeare edition (2001).

THE QUESTIONS

Whenever you come across a question in the guide with a star ✪ in front of it, think about it for a moment. You could make a few notes to focus your mind. There is not usually a 'right' answer to these: it is important for you to develop your own opinions if you want to get an 'A'. The 'Test' sections are designed to take you about 15–20 minutes each – time well spent. Take a short break after each one.

OTHELLO

KEY TO ICONS

A **theme** is an idea explored by an author. Whenever a theme is dealt with in the guide, the appropriate icon is used. This means you can find where a theme is mentioned by flicking through the book. Go on – try it now!

Love and sex

Jealousy and envy

Appearance and reality

Race and otherness

The individual and society

STYLE AND LANGUAGE

This icon is used in the Commentary wherever there is a special section on the author's choice of words and imagery.

CONTEXT

Shakespeare's sources

Shakespeare took the plot for *Othello* from a story in Giraldi Cinthio's collection of tales, *Hecatommithi* (1656). In Cinthio, 'Disdemona' does not elope with Moor (who is not named); her family reluctantly agree to the marriage, and the couple live happily in Venice. The Moor is given the command of Cyprus. He and Disdemona sail there together (not separately). The Moor's junior officer, 'the Ensign' falls in love with Disdemona, but she is not interested in him. He thinks this must be because she loves 'the Corporal' (Shakespeare's Cassio), and therefore plots revenge on Disdemona and the Corporal (rather than the Moor). The Ensign (not his wife) steals the handkerchief. The Corporal finds it in his house and tries to return it, but hurries away when he hears the Moor's voice. The Ensign persuades the Moor that Disdemona is having an affair (as in *Othello*), but it is he, not the Moor, who bludgeons her to death with a sandbag. Both men then make the roof fall on her so that it looks like an accident. (By this time, the Ensign has attacked the Corporal, slicing through his leg.) The Moor regrets the murder and strips the Ensign of his rank (as Othello does Cassio). In retaliation, the Ensign tells the Corporal that it was the Moor who cut his leg off. In the end the Moor is exiled, then killed by Disdemona's family. The Ensign is tortured to death for another crime. His wife survives to tell the tale (unlike Emilia).

It is worth reading the original (which is quite short) to see what Shakespeare has changed. It is included as an Appendix in the Arden edition of *Othello* (and summarized in its introduction). Shakespeare adds depth of character, and poetry, but he also makes plot changes. Some can be explained by theatrical practicalities: it would be hard to have a roof collapse on Desdemona's head every night! In addition, Roderigo is Shakespeare's invention; so is the deep resentment that Iago feels towards Othello, and the professional envy he feels towards Cassio. The handkerchief takes on a deeper significance in Shakespeare's play.

A few of Shakespeare's lines can be better understood in the light of Cinthio's story. At the end of Act 2, scene 1, Iago says of Desdemona *Now I love her too*. This seems odd, since he never mentions it again, but it can be understood as a leftover from Cinthio. Similarly, in Act 5, scene 1, the wounded Cassio complains *My leg is cut in two*. We assume from Shakespeare that Cassio, in his distress, is exaggerating. However, in Cinthio, the Corporal's leg really is cut off, and he has to wear a wooden one.

Shakespeare probably got some of his information on Venice from Lewkenor's translation of Cardinal Contarini's *Commonwealth and Government of Venice* and used Holland's 1601 translation of Pliny's *Natural History* for Othello's exotic background, with its mentions of cannibals, Anthropophagi, the Pontic Sea, and chrysolite. Another work Shakespeare probably consulted was John Pory's translation of John Leo's *A Geographical Historie of Africa*. Leo was a Moor, brought up in Barbary. Interestingly, in the light of Othello's character, Leo writes of his countrymen: 'Most honest people they are, and destitute of all fraud and guile', 'very proud and high-minded, and wonderfully addicted unto wrath ... Their wits are but meane, and they are so credulous, that they will beleeve matters impossible which are told them'; 'No nation in the world is so subject unto jealousie.' In addition, some details of Othello's life may be taken from Pory's biographical note on Leo.

Genre

Othello is a **tragedy** (play featuring a noble hero who eventually dies through a fatal weakness, coupled with fate). It has been called a **domestic tragedy**, and it may have been influenced by other plays of this type, especially *Arden of Faversham* (1592) and *A Warning for Fair Women* (1599), both anonymous. However, it is also a **revenge tragedy**, as was *Hamlet*. This was a popular Elizabethan and Jacobean dramatic **genre** (literary form). The genre is characterized by secret plotting and trickery, and of course by violent revenge murders occurring at the end of the play.

CONTEXT

Another factor relating to genre is that in some ways Iago conforms to a contemporary character type, the 'malcontent'. The hero of *Hamlet* is another such malcontent, but one whose disenchantment with the world tends more towards philosophy than evil scheming. However, the two characters mirror each other: Hamlet rationalizes putting off a deed from which he recoils; Iago rationalizes doing a deed to which he is attracted.

Moors in London

John Leo's dedication refers to what was probably a non-literary source for Shakespeare: the Ambassador of the King of Barbary (see illustration, page 3) arrived in London with his staff for a six-month stay in August 1601. These exotic visitors caused a stir, and Shakespeare himself probably saw them, and perhaps even spoke to them or performed before them. In Elizabethan England racism had not yet taken root as it did when the slave trade became more widespread, although there were enough black men and Arabs in London to cause a degree of racist reaction, as an official document shows:

> 1601. Negroes and Blackamoors. Whereas the Queen's Majesty is discontented at the great number of 'negars and blackamoores' which are crept into the realm since the troubles between her Highness and the King of Spain, and are fostered here to the annoyance of her own people ... In order to discharge them out of this country, her Majesty hath appointed Caspar Van Zeuden, merchant of Lubeck, for their transportation. (Arden edition, p. 29)

Venice and Cyprus

Shakespeare may have met Venetians in London, and he had access to books about Venice (see above). Venice was an independent state with several colonies, although it was already beginning to decline as an international power. Its principal rival, as in *Othello*, was Muslim Turkey, although it was also a trade rival to Britain. It was regarded as a sophisticated materialistic culture, as well as being a place of pleasure – especially sexual pleasure. Its women were thought

CONTEXT

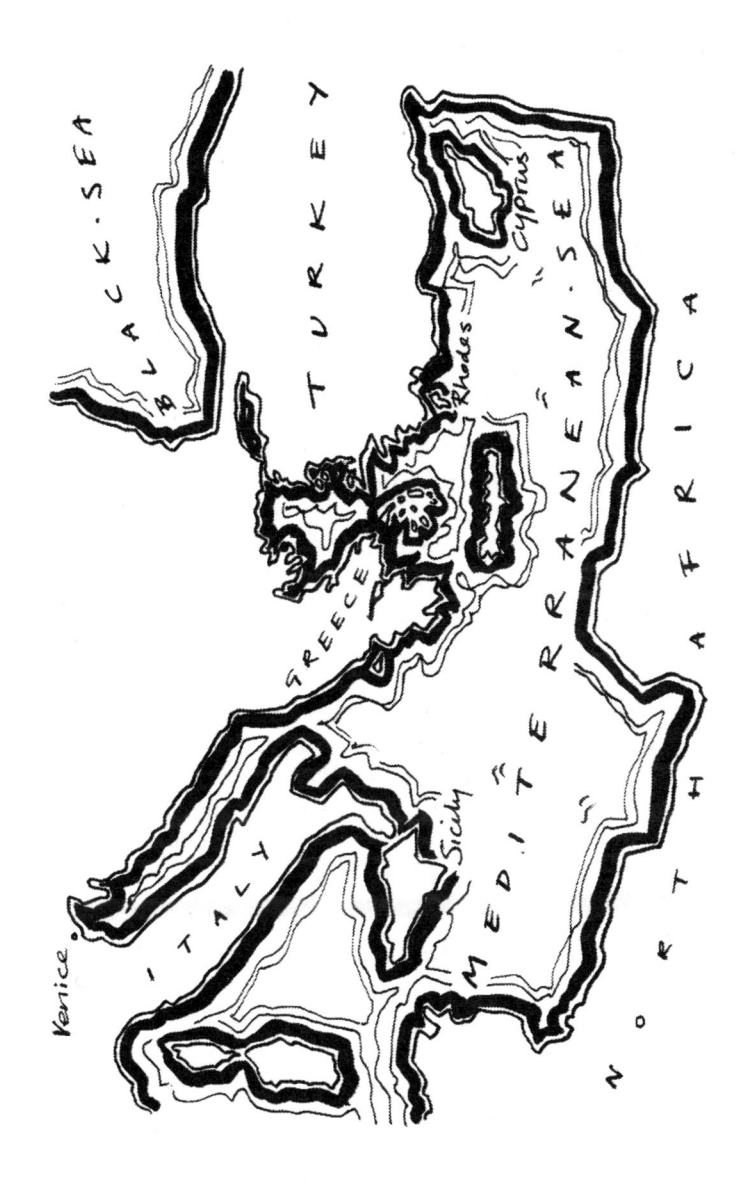

of as elegant, beautiful, but unfaithful. Hence Iago, a Venetian, can worry Othello by claiming that he knows them better than he does.

Cyprus as delineated in *Othello* could be any Mediterranean island. The important thing is that it is seen as half-way between 'civilized' Europe and 'savage' Africa and Asia. One point not mentioned by Shakespeare, however, may be relevant. It was associated with Aphrodite (Venus), goddess of love, and therefore an appropriate setting for a love story – even a tragic one.

Dating and texts

Othello was written between late 1601 and 1604, probably between *Hamlet* and *King Lear*. We know that it was performed at court in 1604, but not necessarily for the first time. Critics vary on their dating of the play, arguing mostly on the basis of stylistic clues (see page 39 for an example).

Shakespeare's text has not survived. However, there are two main versions of the play printed in early editions of his plays published after his death in 1616. The Quarto text (referring to the small square pages), published in 1622, was based on theatre notes and actors' memories. The First Folio (1623) differs from the Quarto in many small ways. For example, it replaces some of Iago's oaths. Modern editors produce their own versions based on these two early versions, and make their own changes if they think that scribes have miscopied in the early versions. See page 73 for an example in which a line can be ascribed either to Desdemona or Emilia.

Test your knowledge and understanding

1 Which *Othello* character does not exist at all in Cinthio?
2 How did Shakespeare know about cannibals?
3 What visit in 1601 probably influenced Shakespeare?
4 What did the English think Venetian women were like?
5 When was *Othello* written?

Look back to check your answers, then take a break.

The Story of *Othello*

Act 1

The play begins on a street in Venice, at night. The foolish but rich Roderigo has been paying Iago (Othello's sergeant) to woo Desdemona for him, but now she has eloped with Othello, a Moor. Together, they wake Desdemona's father, Brabantio, to tell him the news. Othello hears that the Duke wishes to see him, but Brabantio arrives and accuses Othello of bewitching Desdemona and tries to have him arrested. They all go to see the Duke.

Meanwhile the Duke and senators hear that a Turkish fleet is heading for Cyprus. While they are considering this, Brabantio arrives with Othello. He repeats his accusation and Othello defends himself. Desdemona is summoned and acknowledges Othello as her lord. The Duke tries to console Brabantio and commissions Othello to defend Cyprus. Desdemona is to follow him there with Iago. Iago persuades Roderigo that he will soon have Desdemona, then works out a plan to ensnare Othello.

Act 2

On Cyprus, Cassio (Othello's lieutenant) reports that a storm has destroyed the Turkish fleet. Iago and Desdemona arrive there, followed by Othello. Iago instructs Roderigo in his plan. Cassio is responsible for the night watch, but Iago gets him drunk. Roderigo provokes Cassio, who drunkenly pursues him and then attacks Montano. Othello sternly dismisses the remorseful Cassio. Iago slyly suggests that Cassio ask Desdemona to plead for his reinstatement.

Act 3

Emilia arranges for Cassio to speak to Desdemona. Cassio sneaks away as Othello and Iago arrive. Iago uses this to plant suspicion in Othello's mind. Desdemona pleads Cassio's case,

OTHELLO

but Othello resists. Later, she drops her handkerchief, which Emilia finds and gives to Iago. Iago gives Othello further 'proof' of Desdemona's infidelity: he has seen Cassio with the handkerchief, and has heard him talk in his sleep as if to Desdemona. Iago works Othello up to a fever-pitch of jealousy. Othello vows revenge and Iago vows to help him.

When Desdemona cannot produce her handkerchief, Othello explains its powers and how much the thought of its loss worries him. Desdemona denies losing it and Othello angrily exits. Emilia suggests that he is jealous. Meanwhile, Iago has planted the handkerchief in Cassio's room, where he finds it. Liking it, he asks his mistress Bianca to copy it.

Act 4

Iago stirs Othello's jealousy to such a pitch that he has a fit. Not content with this, Iago stage-manages further 'evidence', getting Cassio into a conversation about Bianca, which Othello spies on in the belief that the woman discussed is Desdemona. As a result Othello decides to strangle Desdemona. Lodovico arrives from Venice with a letter for Othello, and when Desdemona mentions Cassio, Othello hits her, to Lodovico's dismay.

Othello questions Emilia, then summons Desdemona and accuses her of falsehood. Emilia and Iago sympathize with Desdemona, Emilia suspecting that some villain has slandered her. Meanwhile, Roderigo begins to suspect that Iago is duping him.

Desdemona prepares for bed, singing sadly and talking with Emilia.

Act 5

Urged by Iago, Roderigo ambushes Cassio, but Cassio is protected by his mail coat and wounds Roderigo. Realizing this, Iago slashes at Cassio's leg from behind. Othello gloats over Cassio. Then Lodovico and Gratiano arrive but are afraid to help. Iago appears as if from his bed, stabs Roderigo and bandages Cassio. When Bianca appears she is distraught at the sight of Cassio wounded. Nonetheless, Iago tries to implicate her in the attack.

THE STORY OF OTHELLO

Othello accuses Desdemona of infidelity and suffocates her. Desdemona revives momentarily and tries to take the blame herself. When Othello admits to Emilia that in fact he killed Desdemona for committing adultery, Emilia fiercely condemns him and cries for help. Montano and Gratiano confront Othello, and Emilia reveals Iago's villainy. Iago stabs her and flees. However, Montano and Gratiano bring him back and Othello wounds him, then kills himself after making a speech expressing his wish that people will not think too badly of him. Iago is condemned to a slow death. Cassio is made governor of Cyprus.

Try this

1. Draw your own picture version of the story. You don't have to be a great artist – visual symbols will do. Keep the Acts divided.
2. Work out what period of time you think the story covers. Then check under 'The timescale' (page 42).

Got your story straight? Then take a break.

CHARACTERIZATION

There are more uncertainties about the characters in *Othello* than in other Shakespeare plays. This fits the general mood of uncertainty in the play. We hear about most characters before we meet them in person, and then have to reassess our impressions of them. There is a great deal of room for personal interpretation, and you should show in your coursework and exam essays that you are aware of this. You should also be prepared to argue your own interpretation, backing it up with examples and quotations from the text.

Othello: *noble but credulous soldier*

If you have studied *Macbeth*, you will remember that Macbeth's reputation goes before him. Even before his first entry, he is described as a brave general, a man of action. Moreover, he is most sure of himself as a loyal soldier serving the state. We also hear about Othello before meeting him in person. However, this is Iago's version of him, which presents Othello as *loving his own pride and purposes*, a man both evasive and full of his own words: *with a bombast circumstance/ Horribly stuffed with epithets of war* (Act 1, scene 1, lines 11–13). In Iago's view, Othello is unfair (in not promoting him) and marries Desdemona only out of lust and greed.

A MAN OF ACTION

When Othello appears we have to reassess our view of him. Like Macbeth, he has earned his reputation as a soldier and general. Also like Macbeth, Othello is on firm ground as a man of action, but gets out of his depth when he strays from this role. As a general, he is respected and relied on by the leaders of Venice, as we see when the Duke greets him: *Valiant Othello, we must straight employ you/ Against the general enemy Ottoman* (Act 1, scene 2, lines 49–50). There is no doubt here: Othello is the man for the job.

CHARACTERIZATION

Othello sees himself as inexperienced outside of the field of battle – and perhaps takes some pride in this: *And little of this great work can I speak/ More than pertains to feats of broil and battle* (Act 1, scene 3, lines 87–8). He goes on to say that he has no grace or skill in speaking, although in fact his speeches show both instinctive oratorical skill and poetic refinement. Later in the scene he assures the Duke that he is used to hardships. The *flinty and steel couch of war* has become to him like a *thrice-driven bed of down* (lines 231–2). ✪ Is he boasting, or merely making light of necessity?

OTHELLO'S NOBILITY

We see Othello's nobility early on. He is calmly confident that the services he has done the state will *out-tongue* the complaints of Brabantio. He also tells Iago (and us) that he is of royal descent, and has earned a personal fortune that makes him an equal match for Desdemona. What's more, he values his bachelor freedom as *the sea's worth*, and is sacrificing it only for love, not for money or rank. When confronted by the angry and insulting Brabantio and his men (Act 1, scene 2), Othello's response is dignified and gently humorous: *Keep up your bright swords, for the dew will rust them* (line 59). His natural authority enables him to keep the peace, as it enables him to restore it after the drunken brawl in Act 2, scene 3. Even in his deluded jealousy, he acts out of what he persuades himself are noble motives, killing Desdemona to prevent her from betraying other men.

VULNERABILITY

The problem for Othello is that stepping out of the soldier's world and marrying Desdemona makes himself vulnerable to his own emotions. Although he is significantly older than her, there is no mention of his being married before, or of any previous relationships. For him, falling in love is a delightful surprise. Desdemona's femininity and the feelings it excites in him are outside his experience. He tells the duke that he is too old to be swayed from duty by lust (… *heat, the young affects/ In me defunct*) or Cupid's *light-winged toys*. But how well does Othello know himself? When he meets Desdemona in

Cyprus (Act 2, scene 2), he is overcome with emotion: *It stops me here, it is too much joy.* A few lines later he admits that she makes him *prattle* and *dote/ In mine own comforts* (lines 195–206). In the next scene he looks forward to making love to her: *The purchase made, the fruits are to ensue:/ That profit's yet to come 'tween me and you* (Act 2, scene 3, lines 9–10).

He is in fact, despite his assurances to the Duke, a passionate man with strong emotions. He is also highly sensual, as we see in his anguished fantasies about Desdemona (see Commentary for Act 3, scene 3) and when he smells her *balmy breath* like a rose on the tree, before murdering her (Act 5, scene 2, line 16).

In addition to his unfamiliarity with women, his passion and his sensuality, Othello is trusting, at least when it comes to Iago. Not devious himself, he fails to anticipate deviousness in others. As Iago puts it: *The Moor is of a free and open nature/ That thinks men honest that but seem to be so* (Act 1, scene 3, lines 398–9).

Othello also has a vivid imagination, so that he easily torments himself with images of Desdemona's supposed infidelity. Iago only has to hint. All this adds up to a fatal recipe. There are, however, key questions which you must ask yourself about how this happens:

- Is Othello naturally jealous, or is his jealousy entirely caused by Iago?
- How is Othello to blame for his own downfall?
- Does he love Desdemona throughout the play?

INCONSISTENCY

In some ways Othello is inconsistent. He is generally open and honest, but he secretly elopes with Desdemona. ✪ Could he ever win her father's approval? He trusts Iago, only doubting him for a moment in Act 3, scene 3, when he demands *ocular proof*, yet he is quick to distrust Cassio. He is easily persuaded by Iago but not by Desdemona (perhaps because he is more used to men than women). Although usually straightforward, he deviously spies on Desdemona instead of confronting her. ✪ Why do you think he does this?

CHARACTERIZATION

❂ How far do you agree with Othello's assessment of himself:

Of one that loved not wisely, but too well;
Of one not easily jealous, but, being wrought,
Perplexed in the extreme (Act 5, scene 2, lines 342–4)?

Iago: *malicious manipulator*

The big question about Iago is – why does he do it? Critics are divided about his motives for ruining Othello. ❂ Take time to consider some possible views on Iago:

- He resents being passed over for promotion.
- He genuinely suspects that Othello and Cassio have slept with Emilia.
- He is plain evil, enjoys creating mischief, and merely seeks to justify his actions.
- He is a traditional stage villain, not intended to be psychologically realistic.
- He is a dramatic 'foil' to Othello.

RESENTMENT

From the play's opening scene we see Iago as dishonest and manipulative. He has been extracting money from the foolish Roderigo in return for winning him the hand of Desdemona. Now Roderigo learns that Desdemona is married, and Iago therefore has to convince him that he hates her new husband, Othello. The reason he gives is that Othello has ignored *Three great ones of the city* who wanted him to make Iago his lieutenant. Othello has instead given the post to Cassio, whom Iago sneeringly calls a *great arithmetician* – a man who lacks Iago's own experience of battle. Iago resents being passed over for the post.

Remember that we cannot believe anything Iago says outside of his **soliloquies** (speeches made by one character alone on stage). Cassio may be more experienced than Iago says. On the other hand, we can tell that Iago is not a noble. He has no fortune; his speech is rough, and usually in **prose** (not in verse); and his wife is Desdemona's servant. Cassio, by contrast, has courtly manners and speaks in verse, and in a way that shows his class and refinement (see Act 2, scene 1).

His being an *arithmetician* suggests that he has the education that Iago lacks – which Iago may also resent.

To understand another dimension of Iago's resentment, you must understand the social context. Shakespeare's plays generally show a respect for nobility and an acceptance of the established social order. Iago is not noble, either by birth or character, and although other characters regard him as honest, no one calls him noble. In fact even the word *honest* applied to him by other characters may signify the patronizing way in which a noble might address or refer to a social inferior.

Iago makes a virtue of being a plain soldier who despises the values of the nobility. To him, love is lust, virtue is worthless (Act 1, scene 3), and reputation – so valued by Othello and Cassio – is *an idle and most false imposition* (Act 2, scene 3, lines 264–5). He claims only to value money, repeatedly telling Roderigo *Put money in thy purse* (Act 1, scene 3). A slighted or insulted noble would offer an open challenge, but Iago's methods are underhand, and therefore ignoble. As Othello's 'ancient' (standard-bearer or ensign – a kind of sergeant) he has risen to as high a rank as someone of his class could expect. Yet he demands more, and thinks he is better than his social superiors – which, in Shakespeare's time would be seen as a dangerous threat to the social order.

JEALOUSY

Iago seems to reveal some of his motives to Roderigo, while at the same time tricking him. Yet it is only in soliloquy that he reveals, or claims, a sexual motive for hating both Othello and Cassio. At the end of Act 1, scene 3, we read:

> *I hate the Moor*
> *And it is thought abroad that 'twixt my sheets*
> *He's done my office. I know not if't be true ...*
>
> (lines 385–7)

The wording suggests that he hates Othello anyway, and that this rumour merely adds to his hatred. It seems he hardly cares whether it is actually true. In Act 2, scene 1 he repeats his suspicion of Othello, but this time adds *... the thought thereof/ Doth like a poisonous mineral gnaw my inwards ...* (lines 294–5). This evocative **image** (word picture bringing an idea to

CHARACTERIZATION

life by appealing to the senses) is more convincing, but a few lines on he casually mentions a similar suspicion about Cassio: *I fear Cassio with my night-cap too.* In Act 4, scene 2, Emilia confirms that Iago once suspected that she had slept with Othello. ○ How genuine are Iago's suspicions of Othello and Cassio?

Whether or not Iago is genuinely jealous, he is unhealthily obsessed with sex, always seeing it in animalistic terms, as something base, rather than as an expression of love. (See 'Themes' under 'Love and sex', pages 24–7.) Despite his disgust, he takes a perverse voyeuristic pleasure in getting other people to imagine sex – notably Brabantio (Act 1, scene 1) and Othello (especially in Act 3, scene 3).

IS IAGO EVIL?

At one level, Iago's dishonesty has rational motives. He fools Roderigo in order to line his own purse; he resents not being promoted and therefore sets out to undo Cassio. However, it does not stop there. He seems determined to ruin Othello by driving him *Even to madness* (end of Act 2, scene 1). He even identifies with hell and the devil:

> *Divinity of hell!*
> *When devils will the blackest sins put on*
> *They do suggest at first with heavenly shows*
> *As I do now.*   (Act 2, scene 3, lines 345–7)

In Act 4, scene 1, Iago suggests to Othello the method for murdering Desdemona. And when Iago is with her in Act 4, scene 2, he shows no sign of pity for her, although she has done him no wrong. This, perhaps even more than his treatment of Othello, Cassio and Roderigo, suggests that Iago is inhuman. We can also see moments when Iago clearly enjoys his destructive scheming, such as at the end of Act 1, scene 3, when he cries *I have't, it is engendered!* as he hits on a plan.

STAGE VILLAIN OR ROUNDED CHARACTER?

It would be hard to argue that Iago is a fully 'rounded' character psychologically, since this would necessitate his having some good points, or at least excuses for his behaviour. In fact there is not a single character in the play who benefits

OTHELLO

from Iago's existence. Othello, Cassio and Roderigo all believe themselves to be indebted to him, when in reality the opposite is true. Despite this lack of psychological realism, Iago does, as we have seen, express some motives. We might also apply a Marxist analysis to the play and say that his class-based resentment is justified. We could even go a step further and speculate on his having sexual problems that have embittered him – although this could only ever be speculation based on the inconclusive evidence of the way in which he talks about sex, and Emilia's apparent discontent with her marriage.

The other approach to interpreting Iago is to see him as a devilish stage villain in the tradition stemming from medieval **mystery plays** (religious plays enacting the story of Christ, with set characters not intended to be realistic). Yet there is no need to decide on one approach over the other. Shakespeare wrote plays that in some ways observe conventions, yet which go beyond them. Therefore Iago can be seen as working on two levels: as three-dimensional character and as stage villain.

A FOIL TO OTHELLO

One last approach to Iago involves seeing the characters of the play as only having significance as part of the whole play. In this dramatic sense, Iago can be seen as existing as a contrast or balance to Othello's virtues. The following table shows this.

Othello	**Iago**
Trustworthy and trusting	Dishonest and suspicious
Indifferent to money (marries for love)	Sees money as the only thing worth having
Passionate	Cold
Direct	Devious
Loves	Hates and despises
Respectful (e.g. Brabantio)	Scornful, dismissive
Grateful, joyful (until Iago corrupts him)	Resentful, bitter
Repents and kills himself	Never repents; remains alive

CHARACTERIZATION

Desdemona: *virtuous victim* ♥

A virtuous young noblewoman, Desdemona's only real misdemeanour in Elizabethan terms is to elope with the man she loves instead of marrying one chosen by her father. This in fact sets two ideals against each other: obedience and love. She chooses love because she has spirit and courage.

That Desdemona loves Othello is without question. She apparently falls in love with him out of pity for the dangers and sufferings of his life, though she probably also identifies with them, as she is a woman of spirit who is denied any outlet for it. In explaining how she came to love him, Othello says: *She wished she had not heard it, yet she wished/ That heaven had made her such a man* (Act 1, scene 3, lines 163–4).

She is young (perhaps about 16) and Othello is old enough to be her father. Therefore it is a mark of her spirit not only that she resists the Duke's proposal that she remain with her father while Othello goes to Cyprus, but that she confidently presses Othello for Cassio's reinstatement in Act 3, scenes 3–4. She is perhaps over-confident, especially as reinstating Cassio would go against Othello's publicly announced decision, and therefore undermine his authority. Perhaps her inexperience of men, and the newness of her marriage, make her insensitive to Othello's reluctance in scene 3 and to his mounting distress about the lost handkerchief in scene 4. She tells a white lie when she says the handkerchief is not lost, but then she may be assuming it will 'turn up'. ◐ How far do you think she is to blame?

In Act 4, Desdemona's innocent virtue is contrasted with Emilia's world-weary willingness to compromise. Desdemona remains devoted to Othello, and swears that she could never betray him, while Emilia admits that she could betray her husband *for all the world*. In Act 5, scene 2, when Othello accuses her of infidelity, and prepares to kill her, she swears her innocence. Twice she tells Othello to send for Cassio and ask him whether Desdemona gave him the handkerchief.
◐ Do you think it is weakness in her that on hearing of Cassio's death she switches to pleading for her life rather than defending herself more forcefully?

17

Cassio: *open-hearted, chivalrous lieutenant*

Like Othello, we first hear of Cassio through the jaundiced view of Iago. Cassio is an educated nobleman – Iago calls him a *great arithmetician*. His manners and speech are courtly, as we see in Act 2, scene 1, when he arrives in Cyprus. Kissing Emilia in greeting he reassures Iago: *'tis my breeding/ That gives me this bold show of courtesy* (lines 98–9). This shows that he sees himself as well-bred, and patronizingly assumes that Iago needs good manners explained to him. He is courtly in his rather fanciful language, but not foppish. In addition, it is in his favour that Othello has faith in him, and that he is concerned for Othello during the storm, and prays to Zeus for his safe arrival. Moreover, even when Othello dismisses him, he expresses no resentment, blaming only himself and the wine he has drunk.

Cassio's conduct towards Bianca is questionable. He treats her lightly rather than badly, but he does not love her and has no intention of marrying her. He complains to Iago that she *haunts* him, and refers to her as a *monkey* and a *bauble* (Act 4, scene 1). It could be argued that his affair with her shows moral weakness, but Shakespeare's audiences would on the whole have excused it. If they blamed him, it would have been for having sex outside of marriage, and with a 'loose' woman, rather than for treating her unkindly.

○ What do you think of Cassio? Will Cyprus be in safe hands with him as its governor?

Emilia: *world-weary but well-meaning wife*

Desdemona's maid Emilia is older and more experienced than Desdemona. Although basically a good woman, life has made her prepared to make moral compromises. Hence she is prepared to take Desdemona's handkerchief in an attempt to please Iago, although she knows that her mistress will be upset if she finds it gone. She also admits to Desdemona that she would be unfaithful in return *for all the world*. This is hardly likely to be on offer, but she is making the point that, for her, fidelity is not a moral absolute. Her attitude is probably coloured by the fact that she is a commoner, and by her rather

CHARACTERIZATION

jaded marriage. Her attitude to Iago suggests that she has hardened herself to his contempt. When he slights her by complaining to Cassio and Desdemona in her presence that she nags him, she replies with restraint, *You have little cause to say so* (Act 2, scene 1, line 108).

Emilia seems devoted to her mistress, although she is at fault for taking the handkerchief and then not confessing to it after Othello has demanded to see it. As Othello becomes more jealous and violent, Emilia is Desdemona's only comfort. She also vigorously defends Desdemona to Othello:

> *I durst, my lord, to wager she is honest,*
> *Lay down my soul at stake: if you think other*
> *Remove your thought, it doth abuse your bosom.*
>   (Act 4, scene 2, lines 12–14)

Later in this scene, after Othello has called Desdemona a *whore*, Emilia is outraged and shows it in her violent wishes for whatever *base notorious knave* has *abused* Othello and made him think this. When Desdemona is dead, Emilia bravely risks her life by berating Othello with what he has done, challenging him, *Do thou thy worst*. When she realizes her husband's guilt, she reveals the truth about him in a passion of moral outrage, with no concern for her own life – and indeed she dies for it. However, perhaps Emilia's most remarkable moment is when she makes her speech in favour of women's rights (Act 4, scene 3, lines 85–102), voicing their grievances and asserting their equality in terms that would not seem proper coming from the innocent Desdemona.

Bianca: *maligned mistress*

Bianca's status is uncertain. Some versions of the play call her 'Cassio's mistress' and others 'a courtesan' (a high-class prostitute). Iago refers to her as a prostitute, and blames her for the attack on Cassio because he knows public opinion will be against her. Emilia regards her in a similar light. However, the evidence of the play shows her only as Cassio's devoted lover, whose only crime is to accept being his mistress rather than his wife.

Bianca shows her devotion by calculating the hours since she last saw Cassio (Act 3, scene 4); she also shows that she is not just a pretty face – by getting the sum right! Her jealousy when she thinks the handkerchief is from another lover is slightly foolish, but hardly surprising given Cassio's offhand attitude. Later (Act 4, scene 1), her language is unladylike: *Let the devil and his dam haunt you!* However, when Cassio is hurt she is distressed and anxious.

✪ How do you think Bianca should be played? How sympathetically should we regard her?

Roderigo: *duped gentleman*

Roderigo in some ways resembles Sir Andrew in *Twelfth Night*: he is easily fooled, has unrealistic romantic hopes, and has more money than sense – for which reason we have little sympathy when he is fleeced by Iago, who quips *Thus do I ever make my fool my purse* (Act 1, scene 3, line 382).

Roderigo believes himself to be in love with Desdemona, but Shakespeare makes him an infatuated fool, a comic butt, rather than someone with whom we might identify. The fact that he is a rich and idle gentleman prepared to trust his wooing to Iago makes him seem fair game. When he says *I will incontinently drown myself* and *It is silliness to live when to live is torment* (lines 306–9), we smile rather than sympathize. He is unlikely to kill himself, since he is rather cowardly.

Roderigo differs from Sir Andrew in that he is not quite harmless. He shares Iago's racism, as we see in the opening scene, and, perhaps more seriously in the Elizabethan context, he is persuaded to pick a fight with Cassio and later to attempt his murder. We are unlikely to feel very sorry when he is killed by Iago (Act 5, scene 1).

Brabantio: *outraged father*

Desdemona's father, Brabantio is a senator, one of the elite group ruling Venice, though probably not in its inner circle. He is both distraught and outraged when finally convinced by Roderigo and Iago that Desdemona has eloped with Othello. Despite welcoming Othello into his home on many occasions, and happily listening to his exciting life-story, when he hears that Othello has married Desdemona he resorts to racist insults and accuses Othello of bewitching her. On the other hand, in the Elizabethan context, it is not so unreasonable that a father should expect her suitor to ask for her hand, and no doubt many fathers of the time would have a similar reaction to Othello's race. ◎ How different do you think this is from modern times?

It is to Brabantio's credit that on the duke's persuasion he resigns himself to the match, and gives his daughter to Othello:

I here do give thee that with all my heart
Which, but thou hast already, with all my heart
I would keep from thee.   (Act 1, scene 3, lines 194–6)

This moment, followed by the touching line, *For your sake jewel,/ I am glad at soul I have no other child*, earns our sympathy, and it seems in keeping when in Act 5 we learn that he has died of a broken heart.

Duke of Venice, Gratiano, Lodovico, Montano

The minor characters of the play represent the Venetian state. The **duke** is a dignified authority figure who encourages Brabantio to make the most of his daughter's marriage to Othello. He even says that his own daughter might have been won by such a tale as Othello's.

Gratiano is Desdemona's uncle. He appears late in the play and with Lodovico discovers the wounded Cassio. He also helps to detain Iago.

Lodovico is a handsome noble sent with papers for Othello from Venice. He serves to voice disapproval and concern when Othello hits Desdemona.

Montano is Governor of Cyprus before being replaced by Othello. Othello mentions his good reputation when he breaks up the fight between him and Cassio (Act 2, scene 3). There is no clear reason for Cassio, rather than Montano, replacing Othello as Governor at the end of the play, except in a dramatic sense, in that it rewards Cassio for his sufferings and defeats one of Iago's aims.

OTHELLO

The Clown is fairly forgettable, and often omitted from productions. He may serve to provide light relief or to give a role to the company's comic actor.

Test your knowledge and understanding

1 In what ways does Othello claim to be an equal match to Desdemona? (Act 1, scene 2)
2 How did Othello win Desdemona's love? (Act 1, scene 3)
3 How does Brabantio help to sow the seeds of Othello's jealousy? (Act 1, scene 3)
4 In what two ways does Iago think Othello has wronged him? (Act 1, scenes 1 and 3)
5 In what way does Iago disparage Cassio's fitness to be Othello's lieutenant? (Act 1, scene 1)
6 Who is Othello's *fair warrior* and why? (Act 2, scene 1)
7 Who does Emilia think should be whipped round the world? (Act 4, scene 2)
8 Why does Iago wound Cassio in the leg? (Act 5, scene 1)
9 Who inherits Othello's property? (Act 5, scene 2)

Your views

1 Some critics suggest that at the end Othello is more concerned with his self-esteem and reputation than with Desdemona's death. How fair is this view?
2 The critic Frank Kermode thinks that Shakespeare himself is confused about Iago's motives. How plausible is this explanation?
3 Is Desdemona entirely blameless in her own death? Make a table or diagram to show her virtues and possible failings.
4 What is the importance of Bianca's role in the play?

Take a break before warming to Shakespeare's themes.

THEMES

The themes of *Othello* could be given as follows:

- Love and sex
- Jealousy and envy
- Appearance and reality
- Race and otherness
- The individual and society

However, there is no absolute agreement on this list, or on its order of importance. For example, some writers might treat 'love' and 'sex' as two different themes; after all, Iago loves no one, yet is obsessed with sex. On the other hand, the love between Othello and Desdemona, even at its most ideal, is based on sexual attraction. Some writers identify jealousy as the main theme, though love and sex are given first place in this guide, as the jealousy which so powerfully motivates Othello is in fact a corruption of his love for Desdemona.

You should also be aware that the themes overlap. For example, sexual love is linked to jealousy. The theme of 'appearance and reality', found in many Shakespeare plays, is linked to that of jealousy, since Othello's jealousy makes him misjudge appearances. Similar connections can be made with other themes. Othello's feelings about his race and status as an outsider make him more vulnerable to Iago's persuasion. This in turn links to the theme of 'the individual and society'. Othello wants to be seen as a Venetian but can never be fully accepted as one.

One could explore the role of women as a separate theme. However, this is dealt with under 'the individual and society' in this guide, partly because it is largely part of the social context of the play, and partly because this issue is only really made explicit in Act 4, scene 3, in a speech made by Emilia.

Love and sex

Several faces of sexual love are revealed in this play. These include: animal lust; 'pure' love; worship (courtly love); and jaded cynicism.

LUST

Iago views 'love' as the mere satisfaction of animal lust. He only ever speaks of male–female relationships in these terms, and his frequent use of animal imagery reflects his view of sex as an expression of base instincts. He pictures the lovemaking between Othello and Desdemona in terms of farm animals mating, and even conjures up a disturbing image of Desdemona *covered by a Barbary horse*. A few lines later, sex is called *making the beast with two backs* (Act 1, scene 1, line 115). When he tells Cassio that Othello has married Desdemona, his imagery – *he tonight hath boarded a land carrack* (a treasure ship) – implies that Othello's motives are financial (Act 1, scene 2, line 50), though a sexual double meaning is also hinted at. Iago is either unable to see love as anything more noble, or else takes a perverse pleasure in degrading what he cannot enjoy himself.

Iago gives his views more explicitly to Roderigo:

If the balance of our lives had not one scale of reason to poise another of sensuality, the blood and baseness of our natures would conduct us to most preposterous conclusions. But we have reason to cool our raging motions, our carnal stings, our unbitted lusts; whereof I take this, that you call love, to be a sect or scion. (Act 1, scene 3, lines 327–33)

He sees base human instincts as only held in check by reason, without which we would be led to ruin (*preposterous conclusions*). So-called 'love' is merely lust – one of these base instincts. His use of *unbitted* refers to the 'bit' that a harnessed horse holds in its mouth, linked to the reins; a *sect or scion* is a cutting from a plant. Nor can Iago conceive of love enduring. He reassures Roderigo that he will soon possess Desdemona by arguing that neither she nor Othello will remain faithful: *It cannot be that Desdemona should long continue her love to the Moor ... nor he his to her* (Act 1, scene 3, lines 342–4).

PURE, RECIPROCAL LOVE

This view is in contrast to that of Othello and Desdemona. Othello describes to the notables of Venice how Desdemona fell in love with him as a result of him telling her his life-story. Rather than presenting love as irrational and accidental (traditionally the work of 'Cupid's arrow'), he gives reasons: *She loved me for the dangers I had passed/ And I loved her that she did pity them* (Act 1, scene 3, lines 168–9). This is a rather neat 'hand in glove' starting point for their relationship. There is reciprocation – a relationship in which each offers something which the other needs. One psychological view is that each of the lovers fulfils the other by living out an undeveloped part of the other's personality. Thus, in Shakespeare's world, a woman had no opportunity for active adventure, but Desdemona can experience this indirectly through Othello. Othello, as a professional soldier who has been fighting since the age of 7, has probably never been pitied. Moreover, Desdemona's femininity represents a total contrast to his familiar man's world.

We see the couple at their happiest in Act 2, scene 1. Tellingly, Othello addresses Desdemona as *my fair warrior*. He is so happy to see her that he can hardly speak. She is his *Honey*, his *sweet*, who makes him *prattle out of fashion, and ... dote/ In mine own comforts* (lines 179–206). Her love for him is as great, but whereas he delights in her femininity, she is obedient and solicitous to his welfare. Even when she irritates him by repeatedly pleading for Cassio's reinstatement (Act 3, scene 3), she is, as she says herself, doing it for his own good. She remains devoted to him as he turns against her. When he explodes in anger and hits her (Act 4, scene 1), her complaint is limited to *I have not deserved this* (line 240). When he dismisses her with *Out of my sight!* she merely answers, *I will not stay to offend you.* Her dying words, when she revives momentarily, are an act of loving self-sacrifice: she risks damnation by lying to protect Othello, telling Emilia that she has killed herself. To the last, she regards Othello as *my kind lord*.

JADED LOVE

The relationship between Iago and Emilia is very different. He claims to suspect that she has slept with both Othello and Cassio, which argues that he feels at least a possessive attachment to her. However, when she brings him Desdemona's handkerchief (Act 3, scene 3), and says *I have a thing for you* he pretends to misunderstand it as an offer of sex, which he dismisses: *it is a common thing*. He toys with her, continuing with word-play: *To have a foolish wife* (lines 305–8). We see their relationship as sour and tired. She steals the handkerchief in an attempt to please him, and indeed the nearest he gets to showing her affection is to say *A good wench, give it me* (Act 3, scene 3, line 317). Act 3, scene 4, line 105 shows her embittered view of men: *They are all but stomachs, and we all but food.* (See pages 29 and 36 for other 'devouring' images.) This is backed up by her 'feminist' speech in Act 4, scene 3. That she is capable of finer feelings, however, is shown by her loyal love for Desdemona, especially in defending Desdemona's name after her death.

COURTLY LOVE

Cassio's view of love is different again. He speaks of Desdemona in courtly terms, almost reverently. He refuses to join in with Iago's sexual banter about her (Act 2, scene 1), and when she arrives on Cyprus he describes her as *divine Desdemona*, whom the elements have allowed to pass safely out of admiration for her beauty. To him, she is the perfect woman. Despite this – or perhaps because of it – he has no sexual intentions towards her. These are reserved for Bianca, for whom he has mild affection but little respect or real love. She, by contrast, despite being presented as a woman of easy virtue, appears to love him more than he deserves, as we see in her long-suffering tolerance of his casual attitude towards her (Act 4, scene 1), and in her real grief when he is hurt (Act 5, scene 1).

THEMES

◯ The critic A.J. Honigmann says that *Othello* is one in a line of Shakespeare plays which show women as being more mature, responsible and faithful in love than men. How far do you agree with his view of women in this play?

Jealousy and envy

Shakespeare incorporated jealousy as a theme in several plays, including *Much Ado About Nothing*, *The Merry Wives Of Windsor*, *A Winter's Tale* and *Cymbeline*. Many critics see *Othello* as a play about jealousy. In a sense, it is, but the jealousy is a corruption of love. It springs from the aspect of love that makes the lover regard the beloved as a possession which they cannot bear to share with someone else. The related emotion of envy is usually stirred by something that the envious person has never had. Iago's envy of Cassio, and perhaps of Othello, is a prime motive for his actions.

IS IAGO JEALOUS?

Iago cites jealousy as his other motive for wanting to ruin Othello:

> *I hate the Moor*
> *And it is thought abroad that 'twixt my sheets*
> *He's done my office* (Act 1, scene 3, lines 385–7)

Some critics are unconvinced by this. Coleridge, notably, saw Iago as essentially malignant, hating Othello without reason and wanting to ruin him out of a love of destructiveness for its own sake. Coleridge saw Iago as 'hunting' for motives to justify his feelings. This view was easier for a predominantly Christian audience to take, as it identifies Iago with the devil (he calls himself a devil in Act 2, scene 2). Modern audiences tend to want psychological explanations. Critics in the Coleridge tradition point out that Iago says *I hate the Moor/ And ...* not 'I hate the Moor, because ...'. In other words, this rumour is only a secondary motive.

Against this view there is Iago's strange soliloquy at the end of Act 2, scene 1, in which he says he loves Desdemona:

OTHELLO

> *... partly led to diet my revenge,*
> *For that I do suspect the lusty Moor*
> *Hath leaped into my seat, the thought whereof*
> *Doth like a poisonous mineral gnaw my inwards ...*
>
> (lines 292–5)

The image he uses here suggests that he really does feel jealous and therefore wants revenge. Moreover, Emilia later refers to his jealousy (Act 4, scene 2).

Another interpretation of Iago, tried out by Laurence Olivier in one stage production, is that Iago has homosexual tendencies and is actually jealous of Desdemona. If this is true, and if he cannot accept his own sexuality, this might explain the disgust he expresses for sex. ❂ How valid an interpretation do you think this is?

IS OTHELLO INNATELY JEALOUS?

Iago himself says Othello is of a *constant, loving, noble nature* (Act 2, scene 1, line 287). Desdemona, ironically, says that Othello is ... *true of mind, and made of no such baseness/ As jealous creatures are* (Act 3, scene 4). She makes an important point here. The Elizabethans thought of jealousy as ignoble. It is therefore Othello's 'tragic flaw' that he is susceptible to jealousy. It may be in fact that he is susceptible to it because of two other character traits: (1) his trusting nature and (2) his imagination.

At the outset he trusts Desdemona completely. He does not seem to react to Brabantio's suggestion that she may deceive her husband as she did her father. Nor does he worry about her travelling to Cyprus in the care of Iago. Indeed he puts complete trust in Iago, choosing to believe his slanders without anything approaching real proof. In addition, it seems he has little experience of women, believes he has found perfection in Desdemona, and has quickly come to depend on her. He has *garnered up* his heart in her; she is *The fountain from the which my current runs* (Act 4, scene 2, lines 58–9). His love for her is based on very high expectations.

The second characteristic making Othello susceptible to jealousy is his imagination. Iago's persuasion from the first follows a strategy of 'less is more'. He has only to hint at

Desdemona's infidelity, and to imply that he could say more, for Othello's imagination to run riot. Iago makes particular use of this technique early on, when he is still sowing the seeds of doubt. The very fact that he says so little makes Othello suspect *some monster in thy thought/ Too hideous to be shown* (Act 3, scene 3, lines 110–11).

THE GREEN-EYED MONSTER

Jealousy itself is portrayed as a monster. For Emilia, *It is a monster/ Begot upon itself, born on itself* (Act 3, scene 4, lines 161–2). She believes that *jealous souls* are simply jealous because they're jealous. She may be referring to Iago and assuming that Othello is the same. Iago himself calls jealousy *the green-eyed monster, which doth mock/ The meat it feeds on* (Act 3, scene 3, lines 168–9). The *meat* is Othello himself, and the *monster* mocks him by debasing his noble self. It is as if the ignoble side of Othello is growing ever larger as it feeds on the rest of him – a repulsive image.

BIANCA AND CASSIO

In Shakespeare, minor characters and **subplots** echo major characters and the main plot. The relationship between Cassio and Bianca is too closely connected to the main plot to be called a subplot, yet the relatively mild jealousy that Bianca feels when she thinks that Cassio has been given the handkerchief (belonging in fact to Desdemona) by another lover echoes, yet contrasts with, Othello's jealousy. Bianca has more reason to be jealous than Othello does, yet she remains devoted to Cassio, whereas Othello turns against the entirely innocent Desdemona.

✪ How genuine is Iago's jealousy? To what extent is Othello a naturally jealous man?

Appearance and reality

The difference between appearance and reality is a major theme in several Shakespeare plays. In *Othello*, Shakespeare seems to set out to raise doubts. From the start, he makes us wonder what is going on, with scenes opening mid-conversation, so that we have to guess at what has gone before. Night-time settings add to the confusion in the first two scenes, in Act 2, scene 3 (the brawl) and Act 5, scene 1 (when Cassio is attacked). In the opening scene Brabantio has to decide whether to believe Roderigo and Iago or to trust in his own view of his daughter. When the leaders of Venice discuss the Turkish fleet, conflicting reports and Turkish strategy leave them uncertain what to believe. This all helps to convey the message that appearances are deceptive.

However, the arch-deceiver is Iago. Everyone – except his wife – sees him as honest and good-hearted. For example Othello calls him *A man ... of honesty and trust* (Act 1, scene 3, line 285). Cassio, whom he has just tricked into losing his post, gratefully calls him *honest Iago*. In fact he is a master of multi-layered deception. He persuades Roderigo that together they are tricking Othello and Cassio, and he tricks Othello by tricking Cassio (Act 4, scene 1, when he gets Othello to spy on the conversation between himself and Cassio). It is only in his soliloquies that we can trust Iago to say what he thinks, and even then we cannot be sure that he is being honest with himself.

It is also worth noting how often what Iago says is a verbal smoke-screen, in which he appears to be saying more than he is, or hints at more than he actually says. The trusting Othello is ill-equipped to deal with such deviousness. For example in Act 3, scene 3:

IAGO	*Men should be what they seem,*
	Or those that be not, would they might seem none.
OTHELLO	*Certain, men should be what they seem.*
IAGO	*Why then I think Cassio's an honest man.*

(lines 129–32)

At one level this is a plot device and Iago is a traditional stage villain. However, his dishonesty is believable, since we are given motives for it and allowed to see into the workings of his mind. At yet another level, through Iago, Shakespeare explores the philosophical question of how we know what we know. This becomes focused on Othello's demand for proof of Desdemona's infidelity. He thinks he has this in the lost handkerchief, the conversation between Iago and Cassio, and

Iago's account of Cassio's dream of Desdemona, but in fact he can no longer judge what is reliable as proof.

It is the uncertainty as much as the thought of Desdemona's infidelity that drives Othello to the edge of madness. When he murders her, he is convinced of her guilt, and the final blow is to discover that he was deluded. He is even denied an explanation. When he asks Cassio to demand of Iago *Why he hath thus ensnared my soul and body*, Iago merely responds: *Demand me nothing. What you know, you know./ From this time forth I never will speak word* (Act 5, scene 2, lines 300–1). Othello is left in the dark, as are we to a large extent.

Race and otherness

Although Elizabethan England was not a multicultural society, there must have been enough non-Europeans in London for a limited racism to emerge (see page 4). However, in writing *Othello*, Shakespeare did not set out to explore racial issues so much as the issue of 'otherness' or what it meant to be a social outsider. Closely linked to this are issues relating to stereotyping, and of what binds us all together as members of the human race.

Othello is an outsider because he is black, and even more so because he is a black man who has risen to high rank and married a white noblewoman. Brabantio seemed to accept him – Othello even asserts that Brabantio *loved* him, but Brabantio's acceptance does not extend to wanting him as a son-in-law. Brabantio's accusation that Othello has bewitched Desdemona is doubly racist: first, it fits the **stereotype** (fixed expectation of one section of society) – the implication being that this is what black men do; second, it suggests that no nice white girl could possibly be attracted to someone of his colour. Both Iago and Roderigo speak of Othello in racist terms, and even Emilia angrily calls him Desdemona's *filthy bargain*.

The result of this limited acceptance is that when Othello begins to doubt Desdemona, his insecurity as a black individual in a white society quickly emerges, and he wonders if Desdemona has had second thoughts because of his race. In fact, she seems colour-blind. Her only comment on Othello's race is that the sun in his home country has burned out such pettiness as jealousy (Act 3, scene 4).

In some ways Othello conforms to the Elizabethan stereotype of the black man. He is trusting (and therefore childlike), sensual, superstitious (about the handkerchief) and passionate to the point of committing murder. On the other hand, he is noble, refined, self-disciplined and reliable. His virtue is undermined by Iago, but in the end he repents and dies honourably.

The theme of 'otherness' is not quite limited to Othello. Iago is an outsider in that he feels socially inferior, which is why he particularly resents the courtly Cassio. Bianca is an outsider because, whether or not she is actually a prostitute, she is a woman having an affair out of wedlock. Because of this, Iago knows that his attempts to blame Cassio's attack on her may succeed because society will be prejudiced against her. Finally, the Turks, who never actually appear but who feature as a threat to Cyprus, are outsiders, being the dreaded non-Christian 'other' in relation to which Christian society defines itself.

The individual and society

Closely related to the 'race and otherness' theme is the wider one of the relationship between the individual and society. People in Venetian (and Elizabethan) society are either accepted or, to varying degrees, rejected. Othello wants to be accepted, and until pressures start to undermine his self-confidence, he mostly thinks that he is. Iago sees himself as spurned by society, in that he has not been made Othello's lieutenant. For Desdemona, obedience first to her father (until she elopes with Othello), and then to her husband, are essential to her role as a woman in Venetian society.

Loyalty and service to the state are highly regarded in *Othello* and in other Shakespeare plays. Othello's tragedy is personal, but it is played out against the backdrop of the Turkish threat to the Venetian colony of Cyprus. An important aspect of the play as a tragedy is that Othello's gradual disintegration makes him incapable of serving the state. Hence private emotions are a threat to the social order, which is eventually made secure by the appointment of Cassio. ✪ How secure do you think Cyprus will be in his hands?

THEMES

The concepts of the individual's 'honour' and 'reputation' in society are also important in the play. When Cassio loses his position for drunken brawling, he is at least as upset about his reputation as he is about any financial loss. Likewise, when Othello fears that Desdemona has been unfaithful, part of his distress is caused by his sense of being dishonoured in the eyes of society. Iago, on the other hand, is a completely dishonourable character and considers reputation to be worth very little in itself.

Try this

1. Make a spider diagram showing all five themes in the notes section at the back. Show examples of how they appear in the play, and show the links between them. Make it as visual as possible.
2. How would you rank the themes in importance, and why?

Time to take a break.

LANGUAGE, STYLE AND STRUCTURE

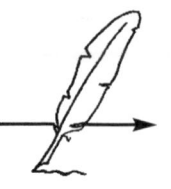

Poetry and prose

Most of the play is written in **blank verse**, which means unrhymed **iambic pentameter** – in which each line consists of five pairs of syllables, each pair containing an unstressed syllable followed by a stressed one. Read a line aloud, stressing the **bold** syllables:

> She **loved** me **for** the **dan**gers **I** had **passed**

Shakespeare varies this a little, mostly to emphasize meaning (see page 63). However, as a general rule, the most regular blank verse is spoken by noble characters who are in a calm and stately mood – for example Othello before he becomes jealous. Prose is often spoken by less noble characters, especially in mundane conversations. An example is when Iago consoles Roderigo in Act 1, scene 3. His down-to-earth advice is best expressed in prose.

OTHELLO

Othello's most stately verse is spoken early on. He makes an impression as a dignified leader of men. The measured and unhurried tone in which he addresses the Senate in Act 1, scene 3 is that of a man used to being listened to attentively. At the same time it is respectful: *Most potent, grave, and reverend signiors,/ My very noble and approved good masters ...*

These early speeches show a command of rhetoric. Notice the formal opening with its triplicity of reverential adjectives in the first line; likewise the unhurried confidence with which he admits to marrying Desdemona, pleads that he is *little blest with the soft phrase of peace* (this very phrase proves that he is being modest!), then lays out the ground he proposes to cover: *I will a round unvarnished tale deliver ...*

As the play goes on, and Othello is influenced by Iago, this commanding style disappears. Othello's lines become tense and clipped: *Not a jot, not a jot ... I will not ... No, not much*

LANGUAGE, STYLE AND STRUCTURE

moved. I do not think but Desdemona's honest. He begins, even here in Act 3, scene 3, to abandon proper sentences. As his mind becomes unhinged, his speech becomes dislocated. The whole speech leading up to his fit (Act 4, scene 1, lines 35–43) is disjointed. Anguished fragments of thought spill out on top of each other, culminating in: *It is not words that shakes me thus. Pish! Noses, ears, and lips. Is't possible? Confess! handkerchief! O devil!*

Only near the end does Othello's speech regain some of its former grandeur. By the time of his 'farewell' speech, leading up to his suicide, his self-possession has returned. This return to dignity is essential for him to qualify as a tragic hero.

DESDEMONA

When Desdemona first appears, in Act 1, scene 3, we might expect her to be daunted by having to answer to her angry father and the Senate, but instead she speaks in a similarly calm, though less inflated style, signifying her attunement with her new husband. When she urges Othello to reinstate Cassio (Act 3, scene 3), her tone is playfully chiding, with short sentences, questions and exclamations. In her final scene, when Othello threatens her life, her short, darting sentences betray her anxiety and mounting desperation.

CASSIO

Cassio is another character with two distinct styles of speech. When he tells Montano about Desdemona (Act 2, scene 1, lines 61–4), he is full of overblown, fanciful praise for her. She is *one that excels the quirks of blazoning pens,* and he personifies nature as being in awe of her beauty. When he is drunk (Act 2, scene 3), all this is lost. He now speaks in plain prose, and merely sounds foolish. When he sobers up, full of remorse, his broken, self-questioning language shows his agitation: *Drunk? and speak parrot? and squabble? swagger? swear? and discourse fustian with one's own shadow?* (lines 275–7).

IAGO

While other characters have one or two modes of speech, Iago has many. While Othello speaks from his emotions, Iago chooses his words and style to fit his purposes. He is deliberately coarse in order to provoke Brabantio. At times he is the no-nonsense soldier, crude but seemingly reliable, as when he advises Roderigo *Put money in thy purse!* (Act 1, scene 3). When he first hints that Desdemona may be unfaithful, he plays the polite, self-critical servant, anxious not to offend or say too much (Act 3, scene 3). At other times he feigns innocence while painting a graphic picture of sexual activity – for example when he describes Cassio's 'dream' or when he considers Othello's demand for proof (Act 3, scene 3). When he vows to help Othello achieve revenge (Act 3, scene 3, lines 465–72), he imitates his master's grand style: Othello swears *by yond marble heaven* and Iago calls on *you ever-burning lights above,/ You elements that clip us round about.* Even in the soliloquies in which he draws us into his murky world Iago can pretend innocence in order to amuse himself, as when he eventually blows apart his own pretence with *Divinity of hell!* (Act 2, scene 3, lines 331–57).

It should be stressed that although Iago is not noble in any sense of the word, his arguments can be sophisticated, and his language sometimes displays a surprisingly educated vocabulary, as well as a vivid imagination. For example his 'love is lust' argument in Act 1, scene 3 includes the line: *The food that to him is as luscious as locusts shall be to him shortly as acerb as colquintida* (line 350; locusts means carob, a sweet food; colquintida is a bitter apple). In the same speech he describes Othello's marriage as *a frail vow betwixt an erring Barbarian and a super-subtle Venetian.*

Shakespeare's imagery

Imagery (the use of word pictures) makes ideas more vivid by giving them a form that appeals to the senses, but the particular choice of image colours the meaning. For example, Iago says his jealousy of Othello *Doth like a poisonous mineral gnaw my inwards.* This **simile** (an image using 'like' or 'as') actually combines two images: a corrosive chemical and a gnawing animal – a chemical with teeth! If Shakespeare had said 'like a hamster gnaw ...', the idea of something eating away at Iago would remain, but without the special nastiness of poison.

LANGUAGE, STYLE AND STRUCTURE

Another point to understand is that if images of a particular kind are used frequently in a play, this helps to build up an **atmosphere** (the emotional feeling generated, preparing us for the action). The use of animal imagery in *Othello* is an example of this (see below).

ANIMALS

Othello, like *Macbeth*, contains a great deal of animal imagery. In both this evokes the animal aspect of human nature, but whereas in *Macbeth* the focus is on men preying on each other, in *Othello* it is on the misery of sexual jealousy. Initially most of this imagery comes from Iago, who uses it more or less deliberately to inflame others. He tells Brabantio that Othello, *an old black ram*, is having sex with Desdemona – *tupping your white ewe* (Act 1, scene 1, lines 87–8). Later he torments Othello with images of Cassio and Desdemona engaged in sex: *prime as goats, as hot as monkeys,/ As salt as wolves in pride*. Othello 'catches' this imagery from Iago, showing that the great man's vision of love is being corrupted, and that in his misery he is sinking to the level of an animal: *I had rather be a toad/ And live upon the vapour of a dungeon* ... (Act 3, scene 3, lines 274–5); *a cistern for foul toads/ To knot and gender in!* (Act 4, scene 2, lines 62–3).

POISON, DISEASE AND MEDICINE

There are other poison images besides the one mentioned in the introduction to this section. These sometimes mingle with images of disease. Iago intends to *pour this pestilence into* [Othello's] *ear* (Act 2, scene 3, line 351). He hopes that his poisonous lies will *with a little art upon the blood/ Burn like the mines of sulphur* (a corrosive mineral). When Othello remember the handkerchief, in Act 4, scene 1, he says *it comes o'er my memory/ As doth the raven o'er the infectious house* (lines 20–1), combining animal and disease in a single image.

These images of poison and disease suggest the insidious way in which Iago gradually corrupts Othello. At the same time, the idea of disease suggests that Othello is infected with Iago's own sickness. Even more sinister is Iago's use of the word *medicine* when Othello has his fit: *Work on/ My medicine, work!* (Act 4, scene 1, lines 44–5), and in his self-satisfied assertion that nothing will ever *medicine* Othello to the *sweet sleep* that he enjoyed before suspecting Desdemona.

MARITIME AND MILITARY IMAGERY

Othello's use of maritime and military imagery conveys a sense of majesty. He says he would not have given up his bachelorhood *For the sea's worth*, had he not loved Desdemona (Act 1, scene 2, line 28). He compares his will to the current of *the Pontic sea* (Act 3, scene 3, line 456). Realizing that his life is nearly over, he says he has reached the *very sea-mark of my utmost sail* (Act 5, scene 2, line 265).

Iago uses maritime imagery far less nobly. He complains that he has been *be-leed and calmed* by Cassio (Act 1, scene 1, line 29) and he refers to Desdemona as a *land carrack* – a treasure ship (Act 1, scene 2, line 50).

ENTRAPMENT

Iago's trickery gives rise to several images of entrapment: *show out a flag* (Act 1, scene 1, line 154); *the net/ That shall enmesh them all* (Act 2, scene 3, lines 356–7); finally Othello's *Will you, I pray, demand that demi-devil/ Why he hath thus ensnared my soul and body?* Some include other elements, especially animal, as in *ensnared*, above, and in the following aside from Iago: *With as little a web as this will I ensnare as great a fly as Cassio. Ay, smile upon her, do: I will gyve thee in thine own courtesies* (Act 2, scene 1, lines 168–70).

LIGHT AND DARK

Another feature that the play shares with *Macbeth* is its use of images of light and dark. The primary one, of course, is in the contrast between *fair* Desdemona and *sooty* Othello. Othello in Act 3, scene 3 calls on *black vengeance*. When Othello contemplates killing Desdemona, he compares it with putting out the light, and afterwards she becomes the *pearl* that he has thrown away (Act 5, scene 2, line 345).

LANGUAGE, STYLE AND STRUCTURE

Dating by style

A feature of *Othello* is its use of **hendiadys**. This is a poetic device in which two related words are used, joined by 'and'. They can either replace a single word, as in *play and trifle with your reverence* (*play* and *trifle* mean almost the same thing) or an adjective and a noun, as in *as loving his own pride and purposes* (instead of 'loving his own proud purposes'). Hendiadys is used frequently in *Hamlet*, and still used at the start of *Othello*, but less so as the play goes on. Thus it helps to establish when *Othello* was written.

Structure

Every Shakespeare play is divided into five Acts, a convention dating from Roman playwrights such as Seneca. It is not possible to generalize much about what happens in each Act in a Shakespeare play, though the groundplan is always set out in Act 1, Act 3 is usually pivotal, bringing conflicts and confusions into the open, and the final climax and resolution always come in Act 5. You may, however, find it helpful to follow the STAR formula outlined below.

THE *STAR* FORMULA

The word STAR here refers to four stages that can be identified in any Shakespeare play, including *Othello*:

1 **S**ituation
2 **T**rigger
3 **A**narchy
4 **R**esolution.

Situation

This means the existing state of affairs at the start of the play. This will usually involve some sort of imbalance, conflict or difficulty which is the 'soil' in which the 'seed' of the play can grow. In *Romeo and Juliet*, the situation is that two families are feuding. In *Othello* it is twofold: (a) the Turks are posing a threat to Venice; (b) Iago hates Othello, and has been getting paid by Roderigo to advance his suit with Desdemona.

Trigger

The trigger is the event that sets off the main action. In *Macbeth* the trigger is Macbeth meeting the Witches. In *Othello* the trigger has already occurred: Othello has eloped with Desdemona. The fact that he has run off with her in secret is already a symbolic dislocation, as is the secret marriage of Romeo and Juliet. Othello has upset Desdemona's father, a member of the Venetian ruling class.

Anarchy

In Shakespeare, there is always a point when the trigger leads to chaos, or anarchy. In *Othello* this takes place largely in Othello's mind, as he is led farther from the truth of Desdemona's innocence into a gross perversion of reality, and even into something approaching madness. At the height of this chaos comes the main climax: the murder of Desdemona. Note that in Act 3, scene 3 Othello says, referring to Desdemona: *... when I love thee not/ Chaos is come again.*

Resolution

The **resolution** is the way in which the play reaches a satisfying ending, allowing the audience to go away with a sense of calm fulfilment. The murder of Desdemona is like a boil being lanced. It immediately causes Emilia to raise the alarm and then reveal the truth. Resolution takes place in Othello realizing at last how wrong he has been about Desdemona, everyone realizing that Iago is a scoundrel, and Othello making restitution in the only way he can now, by taking his own life.

An important aspect of this resolution is the restoration of social order. *Othello* has been described as a 'domestic tragedy', but Othello's personal problems do put Cyprus in danger. In *Macbeth* the social order is restored when Malcolm becomes king; in *Othello* it is important that Othello, no longer fit to govern Cyprus, is replaced by someone regarded as 'a safe pair of hands', namely Cassio.

LANGUAGE, STYLE AND STRUCTURE

SETTINGS

The play has two settings: Venice and Cyprus. Act 1 takes place in Venice. Here, things are relatively safe, although trouble is brewing in the form of the Turkish threat to Venetian power, and Iago's hidden threat to Othello. In Act 2, the action moves to the frontier island of Cyprus, symbolically a half-way point between civilization and savagery. The isolated island setting helps to create a sense of claustrophobia.

Beyond the shift from Venice to Cyprus, the stage directions are vague about settings, though several scenes take place at night, which is fitting for 'dark deeds': the opening, when Iago rouses Brabantio; the drunken brawl involving Cassio; the attack on Cassio and murder of Roderigo; and the murder of Desdemona.

SOLILOQUIES

In other Shakespeare tragedies, the tragic hero is given more soliloquies in which to gain our sympathy and explain his mental processes. These are especially likely to occur early on before the action speeds up in the 'Anarchy' phase of the plot. Macbeth's speech when he weighs up whether or not to murder Duncan is an example. In *Othello* the big soliloquies come from Iago, at the end of Act 1, scene 3, and Act 2, scenes 1 and 3. Othello gets shorter soliloquies in the middle of Act 3, scene 3 and in Act 5, scene 2 (when Desdemona is asleep). This distribution has the effect of giving more power to Iago. The pattern in the scenes in which he gives his soliloquies is that gradually everyone exits except him, as if layers of illusion are peeled off one by one, revealing the nasty truth in the shape of Iago. Remember that for most of the play he is the one character who knows exactly what is going on. (There are some similarities here between him and Macbeth.)

Iago's soliloquies have the effect of drawing us into his world, so that we see things from his point of view – which can be an uncomfortable experience. (This effect is achieved particularly well in the film in which Kenneth Branagh plays Iago.)

THE TIMESCALE

The absence of any real subplot adds to the confined feeling of the play. It also helps events to move fairly swiftly. From the arrival on Cyprus, danger marches quickly, and largely undetected, towards Desdemona, Cassio, Roderigo and Othello. In this respect, Act 3, scene 3 is pivotal. At the beginning of this scene, Othello and Desdemona are still happily in love, and Cassio is hopeful that Desdemona will get his post back for him. But the scene ends with Othello vowing to kill Desdemona, and Iago vowing to help him and promising to kill Cassio – in return for which Othello makes Iago his lieutenant.

When we watch *Othello* on stage, the action marches on towards its tragic close. However, there are two time schemes at work in the play. In the 'short' time scheme, Othello and Desdemona leave for Cyprus the day after their marriage. Cyprus is about 2,200 kilometres from Venice, so it would take several days to sail there (Shakespeare gives no indication of how many). From the arrival in Cyprus until the end of the play is only about 33 hours. They land on Saturday afternoon and Desdemona dies on Sunday night. This speed is needed for dramatic pace, and also because things must move quickly for Iago's scheme to succeed. The longer it takes, the more chance there is of his being found out.

On the other hand, several details give evidence for a 'long' time scheme: Othello claims that Desdemona and Cassio have had sex *A thousand times* (Act 5, scene 2, line 210); Emilia says that Iago has asked her *a hundred times* to steal the handkerchief (Act 3, scene 3, line 296); Bianca complains that Cassio has been away for a whole week (Act 3, scene 4, line 173); Roderigo, a rich man, has just arrived in Cyprus but has already spent all his money (Act 4, scene 2, lines 87–8).

Shakespeare's source, Cinthio, spreads events over a longer period of time. It follows that Shakespeare's use of the short time scheme was deliberate. The fact that it is interwoven with traces of a longer timescale could suggest simple inconsistency. However, some critics, such as Honigmann (see Arden edition, pp. 68–72), believe that the double scheme is deliberate, cleverly combining the need for pace with the need

LANGUAGE, STYLE AND STRUCTURE

for credibility: it is hard to believe in Othello moving from blissful love to jealous murder in 33 hours!

Mind your language!

1 What are the features of 'iambic pentameter'?
2 How does Othello's language change as the play progresses?
3 What characterizes Iago's language?
4 What are the main five types of imagery in the play?
5 What does the mnemonic STAR stand for?
6 What is the main trigger to the action of *Othello*?
7 What are the two settings in *Othello*?
8 Who gets the most soliloquies in the first three Acts?
9 How many timescales are at work in the play?

Look back for the answers and then take a break before the Commentary.

COMMENTARY

Act 1, scene 1

- ◆ Roderigo protests to Iago that Desdemona has married Othello.
- ◆ Iago insists he didn't know, and that he hates Othello.
- ◆ They awaken Brabantio and persuade him that his daughter has eloped with Othello.
- ◆ Brabantio sets out to find his daughter and Othello.

The scene is set at night, on a street in Venice. The night setting helps to create an atmosphere of uncertainty. The abrupt opening pitches us straight into the action and makes us ask questions. What is it that Roderigo accuses Iago of not telling him? Who is it that Iago says he hates? Iago immediately gives his reasons: the mystery man has ignored recommendations to make Iago his lieutenant, instead appointing Michael Cassio. Iago sneers at Cassio as someone who knows only about the theory of war, whereas he, Iago, is an experienced and proven soldier. At the end of this speech we discover that the man he hates is 'the Moor': significantly, Othello is first identified not by his name, but by his race.

Iago assures Roderigo that he follows Othello merely for his own advantage, not out of loyalty. In fact he despises loyal servants who dote on their *obsequious bondage* like asses. Like Edmund in *King Lear*, and like the traditional stage villain, Iago reveals his contempt for the established order and for conventional virtue. Iago is loyal to no one.

The pair must already be near Brabantio's house at the start of the scene, as they now proceed to wake him, shouting up to his window from the street below. (This may stem from *charivari*, an old custom whereby someone objecting to a neighbour's marriage would go and cause a disturbance outside their house.) Iago takes the lead, though in theory acting on Roderigo's behalf. Roderigo is respectful, but Iago enjoys horrifying the old man with vulgar and racist

COMMENTARY

allusions to the fact that Othello may at this moment be having sex with Desdemona. Iago's animal imagery shows his contempt for Othello, for human nature in general, and possibly for sex: *Even now, now, very now, an old black ram/ Is tupping your white ewe!*

Look out for animal imagery throughout the play. You will see that at first it is Iago who uses it, but that Othello 'catches' it from him. In another racist jibe, Iago compares Othello to the devil. Later in the scene he even interrupts Roderigo's polite overtures to put the matter more bluntly, again using racist animal imagery for sex: *Zounds, sir ... you'll have your daughter covered by a Barbary horse.* 'Barbary' is an old name for North-West Africa, from which Iago supposes Othello to have come.

Brabantio's reluctance to believe that Desdemona has eloped is a precedent for the questions of evidence and credulity that abound throughout the play. The theme of class also emerges here. Brabantio calls Iago a villain, but, since Iago is in fact no gentleman, instead of responding to this insult with a challenge, he responds only with veiled sarcasm: *You are a senator!*

Roderigo again puts the matter politely but with some urgency, invoking the stereotype of the *lascivious Moor*, and eventually Brabantio is persuaded to take action. When the old man disappears briefly, we learn that Iago does not expect the elopement to lead directly to Othello's downfall, as the state needs him too much. However, he hopes it will *gall* him – earn him a stinging reprimand.

When Brabantio reappears, Iago has gone, aware that it will not look good for him to be involved in exposing his own master. Brabantio asks Roderigo if he thinks Othello may have bewitched Desdemona – a theory which Roderigo encourages. The scene ends with Brabantio gathering a force to apprehend Othello.

Act 1, scene 2

◆ Othello and Iago discuss Brabantio's reaction to Othello's marriage.
◆ Cassio brings word that the Duke wishes to see Othello.

OTHELLO

- ◆ Brabantio accuses Othello and tries to have him arrested.
- ◆ Othello points out that he has been summoned by the Duke.

Again, we begin with uncertainty, in mid-conversation. Iago, very much in character as a deceiver, tells Othello that only his conscience has prevented him from killing someone who has spoken in *scurvy and provoking* terms about Othello. However, we cannot be sure whether Iago refers to Roderigo or Brabantio.

Othello is confident that in the eyes of the authorities his services to Venice will outweigh his offence to Brabantio in eloping with Desdemona. He asserts that he is an equal match to her in fortune and rank – in fact he is of royal blood. Moreover, only love for Desdemona has made him give up his bachelor freedom. His use of the word *unhoused* suggests that as a soldier he has lived much of his life outdoors.

Cassio comes to fetch Othello to the Duke on business relating to Cyprus. As so often in Shakespeare, and in this play, state affairs reflect private concerns. There is a confused threat to Venice's power in Cyprus, while at the same time there is a threat to Othello in the form of Brabantio. In both cases, the facts are disputed, but there is a general sense of urgency.

When Othello exits, Iago can talk to Cassio in a less loyal and more vulgar tone, using maritime imagery to tell Cassio that Othello has married a fortune – *boarded a land carrack* (a treasure ship). Iago breaks off the conversation with Cassio the moment Othello returns, knowing that his master would disapprove – and probably enjoying the opportunity to tantalize Cassio by not revealing the name of Othello's bride.

With the entry of Brabantio the action takes on a new dynamic. Picture the three groups now onstage: Othello and his attendants, Cassio and the officers, and Brabantio – again, with officers. The latter two groups both want Othello for quite different reasons. There is confusion, accentuated by the night-time setting, and there is the threat of violence, which Iago immediately uses to his own advantage by challenging Roderigo. ✪ Why do you suppose he does this, and how should the actor playing Roderigo react?

COMMENTARY

✒ Amidst this confusion, Othello shows his calm dignity and self-confidence with three lines of fine poetry aimed at keeping the peace:

Keep up your bright swords, for the dew will rust them.
Good signior, you shall more command with years,
Than with your weapons.

Notice the simplicity of these lines, especially the first, which is composed of single-syllable words. These are the words of a man who feels no need to impress with overblown language. Othello shows a gentle respect for Brabantio's age, despite the old man calling him a thief. Nonetheless, Brabantio seems unmoved. He angrily accuses Othello of enchanting Desdemona, binding her *in chains of magic*. His argument is a racist one: (1) Othello is black and therefore damned and likely to use black magic; (2) Desdemona, previously opposed to marriage, would not run to *the sooty bosom* of a *thing* like Othello, a black man, had she not been charmed or drugged. Ignoring this racist slur, Othello keeps the peace, calmly pointing out that if he goes to prison he cannot go to the

Duke, who has summoned him on *present business of the state*. The scene ends without blows being exchanged.

Act 1, scene 3

- The Duke and senators hear that a Turkish fleet is heading for Rhodes, then Cyprus.
- Brabantio asserts that his daughter has been bewitched – and by Othello.
- Othello defends himself.
- Desdemona is summoned and acknowledges Othello as her new lord.
- Brabantio resigns himself to the marriage.
- The Duke commissions Othello to defend Cyprus.
- It is agreed that Desdemona will follow Othello to Cyprus with Iago.
- Iago reassures Roderigo, then works out a plan to ensnare Othello.

'MY DAUGHTER, O MY DAUGHTER!'

The mood at first is urgent but businesslike. Yet the uncertainty generated by the conflicting reports and the Turkish subterfuge (*a pageant/ To keep us in false gaze*) anticipates that which Iago will create in Othello. Conflict comes closer to home on the entry of Othello and Brabantio. Notice that Othello is twice called *valiant* and that the Duke fails to see Brabantio at first, suggesting that Othello's position is the stronger of the two. ✪ How might a director emphasize this on stage?

Brabantio's cry of *My daughter, O my daughter!*, echoes other aggrieved fathers in Shakespeare, including Capulet in *Romeo and Juliet* and Shylock in *The Merchant of Venice*. ✪ Is Brabantio seeking to protect or control Desdemona? He repeats his argument that she must have been bewitched. There is an interesting moment dramatically when the Duke, having given Brabantio the authority to pronounce sentence on the culprit, *Who'er he be*, learns that the accused is Othello. The tension here is between private loyalty and the needs of the state. The Duke will be reluctant to imprison the man he needs for the defence of Cyprus.

Othello presents himself as a rough soldier, *little blessed with the soft phrase of peace*, but even his explanation reminds us, and the Duke, why Venice needs him: he has been fighting battles since the age of 7! With confident irony he promises to reveal *what mighty magic* he has used on Desdemona. The Duke's refusal to be led by the weak evidence *Of modern seeming* (commonplace appearance) may be an appeal against racial prejudice.

On Othello's request, the Duke sends for Desdemona. Notice that her name has not been mentioned in this scene, yet the Duke knows it. This shows that Brabantio is close to the Duke, and perhaps that the leading Venetians are almost like a private club – one from which Othello is excluded, however much he is sought after for his skills.

In a key speech, Othello explains how Desdemona fell in love with him by hearing about his hardships and adventures. Even in this account we see what some critics

COMMENTARY

have called Othello's self-dramatization. The wonders he claims to have seen, such as *Anthropophagi* (cannibals), are fantastic, and in themselves make him interesting. In addition, he is of course the hero of the *moving accidents* and *hair-breadth scapes* that he mentions. In explaining Desdemona's love, he glorifies himself.

Notice that Othello begins this speech with the words *Her father loved me*. This shows either that Othello is naive, or that Brabantio loved him as a storyteller but not as a son-in-law. Also note Othello's account of Desdemona's reaction. She wishes *That heaven had made her such a man*. To some critics, this suggests that Desdemona has an active, adventurous side to her character that she cannot easily express as a woman of her time, and which she feels is expressed in Othello, which therefore attracts her to him.

Desdemona's first words, *My noble father,/ I do perceive here a divided duty*, reveal her to be a respectful and perceptive young woman. She points out that her first duty is now to her husband, after which her father reluctantly gives her to Othello, acknowledging that in fact she is already his. Bitter though Brabantio is, he still calls Desdemona *jewel*.

The Duke seeks to console Brabantio in a speech composed of rhyming couplets, each sounding like a proverb. His message is: what's done is done; make the most of it. Brabantio answers in similar couplets, ironically comparing his loss with the possible loss of Cyprus. His 'proverbs' *sugar* (sweeten) and *gall* (embitter) in equal measure. (They are equivocal.) His final couplet means that mere words offer no real comfort. His last line falls into prose, signifying the return to matters of state.

BACK TO THE TURKS

Othello, told that he must *slubber the gloss* (spoil the shine) of his new marriage by going off on this military expedition, says that he is no stranger to hardships and has no problem putting up with them. Again, this could be seen as self-dramatization – bragging about how tough he is. However, he asks for Desdemona to be looked after. Brabantio rejects the Duke's suggestion that she stay at her father's house, as does Othello.

OTHELLO

Interestingly the Duke asks Desdemona what she wants. She argues that if she is left behind, she will be deprived of *The rites for which I love him*, by which she probably means the 'rites' of war, though she may mean the marriage rites (rights) – sex. ✪ How valid is this interpretation in your opinion? She does show independence in opting to go against custom and accompany her husband to war.

Othello backs her, insisting that he does so not in order to satisfy his own sexual desire, but *to be free and bounteous to her mind*. It is ironic that he seems so liberal now, yet becomes so overbearingly jealous later. He goes on to insist that the *light-winged toys* of love will not distract him from defending Cyprus. Persuaded, and aware of the urgency of the matter, the Duke leaves it up to Othello, and it is arranged for Desdemona to follow after him with Iago. This is one of several occasions when we see how wrong Othello is about Iago, whom he calls *A man ... of honesty and trust*.

The first hint of the jealousy to come is contained in Brabantio's ominous parting shot, warning Othello that Desdemona may deceive her husband as she deceived her father, and in Othello's response: *My life upon her faith*. (He would stake his life on her fidelity.)

'PUT MONEY IN THY PURSE'

Iago is now left to deal with Roderigo, who shows his weakness by threatening to drown himself for love of Desdemona. Iago quips unsympathetically that he will not love him anymore if he does. Iago's tone is cynical and mocking. He gives Roderigo blunt, 'manly' advice to make him pull himself together, telling him repeatedly to *Put money in thy purse*. We see some of Iago's typical animal imagery when he says that he would rather be a baboon than drown himself for a guinea-hen, which could mean a prostitute and at any rate is unflattering to Desdemona. Baboons were thought to be lecherous.

Note that this conversation is in prose, as befits its down-to-earth, unrefined tone.

Iago scorns Roderigo's mention of *virtue*, retorting *a fig!* (traditionally accompanied by an obscene gesture). His speech insisting that we are what we make of ourselves is like a mock sermon: such gardening metaphors are often used in the Bible.

COMMENTARY

Iago is insisting that Roderigo can overcome his love-sickness by an act of will. He goes on to voice the popular stereotype: *These Moors are changeable in their wills* – so Othello will tire of Desdemona, who herself will soon want a younger man than Othello. In short, Roderigo will soon *enjoy her*.

IAGO JEALOUS?

The focus now narrows to Iago, alone in the spotlight. He immediately expresses his contempt for Roderigo (*such a snipe*). It is also in this important soliloquy that Iago gives a second motive for plotting against Othello (the first being Othello's appointment of Cassio), namely that it is rumoured that Othello has had sex with Emilia. Iago, unlike Othello, is not bothered by the lack of proof.

Iago now focuses on how to achieve his twin purposes – to get Cassio's place and to ruin Othello. Picture him pacing the stage, racking his brains (*How? How? let's see ...*). We see his mind at work as he considers how to play on Othello's *free and open nature*, until in delighted triumph he exclaims *I have't, it is engendered!* Characteristically, the image he uses for his scheme is sexual (*engendered* refers to impregnation by the sexual act). The joint midwives of this monster (his plan) are Hell and night.

Act 1: test your knowledge and understanding

(Answers at end of Commentary, page 84)

1. Why is the opening scene set at night?
2. Why is Othello not referred to by name at first?
3. Who refers to whom as *an old black ram*, and what is the significance of this image?
4. Of what does Brabantio accuse Othello, and why?
5. What does Othello's poetic response to Brabantio show?
6. How do Turkish tactics help to establish the mood of the play?
7. How does Othello say he won Desdemona's love?
8. How does Brabantio sow a seed of jealousy?
9. What motives does Iago give for hating Othello?

OTHELLO

Your views

1 How noble is Othello so far?
2 How perfect is Desdemona?
3 How convincing are Iago's motives?
4 What evidence could you use to back up your views?

The seed is sown. Take a break to let it grow.

Act 2, scene 1

- Cassio reports that a storm has destroyed the Turkish fleet.
- The ship carrying Iago and Desdemona arrives at Cyprus.
- Iago banters with Desdemona.
- Othello arrives safely.
- Iago instructs Roderigo in his plan to get Cassio dismissed.

STORMY SEAS

The scene takes place somewhere near the coast of Cyprus. A fierce storm has been taking place. Montano, the governor whom Othello is coming to replace, questions whether any ship can hold together under such mountainous seas. A gentleman comments that he has never before seen such *molestation ... On the enchafed flood* (the enraged sea). As elsewhere in Shakespeare (for example *Twelfth Night* and *The Tempest*), wild sea storms foreshadow confusion and disorder in the human world. Although Cassio brings the good news that the storm has destroyed most of the Turkish fleet, dramatic tension is kept up by concern for the ships bearing Othello and Desdemona.

Although Montano is being replaced by Othello, he seems as worried as anyone about Othello's safety, asking *Is he well shipped?* Short speeches keep up the mood of tense anticipation, and good news arrives tantalizingly, first with the sighting of a sail, then with a [cannon] *shot of courtesy*, indicating that the ship sighted is friendly, and finally with the actual arrival. While we wait, Cassio finds time to tell

COMMENTARY

Montano that Othello has married *a maid/ That paragons description and wild fame*. This speech shows that Cassio almost worships Desdemona – which may be innocent enough, but which will make it easier for Iago to use him.
✪ Notice Cassio's courtly language. How does it compare with Iago's?

When the ship bearing Desdemona sails in, Cassio admiringly asserts that the seas, winds and rocks themselves have given safe passage to *The divine Desdemona* out of respect for her beauty. Cassio prays to *Great Jove* (Jupiter) to bring Othello swiftly to shore to *Make love's quick pants in Desdemona's arms*.

♥ These words may be meant sexually, but bear in mind that elsewhere Cassio always speaks respectfully of both Othello and Desdemona, and later refuses to go along with Iago's sexual imagery for Desdemona.

Cassio kisses Desdemona and Emilia, explaining that he does so out of courtesy. Iago responds with a joke at Emilia's expense, implying that she nags him. He goes on to slander women generally, including Desdemona. His line *You rise to play, and go to bed to work* is a veiled sexual insult. Some commentators have criticized the banter which follows between him and Desdemona as being improbable, especially since Desdemona is meant to be worried for Othello's life at this point. However, she does say, *I am not merry, but I do beguile/ The thing I am by seeming otherwise*, suggesting that she is putting on a brave face. Moreover, the passage does

♥ show Iago's inventiveness. Some commentators think it shows that Desdemona understands his sexual innuendo, and is therefore not entirely innocent. ✪ What do you think the passage shows about Desdemona, and about Iago?

In an aside Iago comments on Cassio's Florentine courtesies to Desdemona, which he intends to use to ensnare him.

A SERPENT IN PARADISE

♥ When Othello arrives and greets Desdemona, their happiness is mutual. The only difference is that whereas Othello thinks he could not be any happier than this, Desdemona insists that their love and contentment will grow. As it turns out, Othello is right; so for those familiar with the plot there is dramatic irony here, especially since his line *It stops me here* (he is choked with joy), foreshadows his strangling of Desdemona.

In an aside, Iago takes up Othello's mention of *discords* with a musical image: the lovers may be *well tuned* now, but he will slacken the strings (as on a musical instrument, or heartstrings) and spoil their harmony. This is an appropriate image, since love is often associated with music. (*Twelfth Night* begins with the line *If music be the food of love, play on*.) After Othello and Desdemona go, Iago once again remains on stage to plot with Roderigo. First Iago sets out to persuade Roderigo that Desdemona has fallen in love with Cassio, arguing that she must quickly tire of a husband who is old, rough-mannered and black, and that Cassio is her obvious choice. When Iago describes Cassio, we detect envy, and in fact the picture that Iago paints of Cassio (*a slipper*[y] *and subtle knave*) could more fairly be applied to himself.

We cannot tell how far Iago believes in the mutual lechery that he claims exists between Cassio and Desdemona, but he may have half-convinced himself, just as he has apparently convinced himself of his own wife's infidelities. Iago gets Roderigo to agree that he will provoke Cassio that night. Then we are left once again with Iago's thoughts.

Iago's soliloquy is a telling one. He claims to believe that Cassio loves Desdemona, and that she probably loves Cassio. In terms of the argument, it is not obvious why he now admits to Othello's *constant, loving, noble nature*, but this testimonial does confirm Othello's virtues for us – especially coming from one who hates him. Iago even says now that he loves Desdemona himself, though he qualifies this by saying that he wants her in order to avenge himself on Othello, *wife for wife*. Failing this, he intends to drive Othello mad with jealousy. Notice how he ends the speech. By *'Tis here, but yet confused*, he means that the plan is in his head but not yet worked out in detail. (An actor might tap his head here.) This points to his methods: he works out a rough scheme and then improvises.

COMMENTARY

Act 2, scene 2

◆ A herald announces feasting.

In this very short scene, separate from scene 1 only because its mood is so different, a herald announces that Othello wants general feasting to celebrate the sinking of the Turkish fleet, as well as his wedding. Presumably *liberty of feasting* means that a holiday will be observed, and perhaps that drunkenness will be overlooked. It is also likely that in Shakespeare's theatre an interval would have followed this scene, so that the invitation, and especially *All offices* [food and drink outlets] *are open*, would apply to the audience as well as the characters.

Act 2, scene 3

◆ Othello charges Cassio with responsibility for the watch.
◆ Iago gets Cassio drunk.
◆ Roderigo provokes Cassio, who drunkenly pursues him.
◆ Cassio attacks Montano when he tries to intervene.
◆ Othello dismisses Cassio.
◆ Iago tells Cassio to ask Desdemona for help, then soliloquizes about his scheme.
◆ Iago reassures Roderigo.

A DRUNKEN BRAWL

Othello tells Cassio to make sure the soldiers on guard do their duty, rather than carrying on the revels of the day. Both have faith in Iago's supervision, since, as Othello says yet again, *Iago is most honest*. Othello takes Desdemona off, probably for them to sleep together for the first time. Hence his closing couplet poetically suggests their union. Iago verifies this when he tells Cassio that Othello *hath not yet made wanton the night with her*. This line establishes Iago's tone. He wants Cassio to join in his loose talk about Desdemona, but Cassio refuses to play Iago's game.

Iago now lays his trap, urging Cassio to join him in a toast to Othello. Cassio, having no head for alcohol, is already slightly drunk on a single cup of diluted wine, so his resistance is low. Moreover they have Othello's marriage to celebrate, and the *gallants* will be disappointed if Cassio refuses. Iago confides in us while Cassio fetches them in. When Cassio returns he has had another drink. His response to Iago's song shows that he is already quite drunk. Notice, too, his drunken repetition of the oath *'Fore God*, and that he gets 'hung up' on the word *exquisite*, applying it to English drinkers and Iago's songs, whereas before he used it for Desdemona's perfect beauty. When he attempts to prove that he is sober, he only makes a fool of himself. ✪ How might an actor play him as the scene progresses?

When Cassio goes outside, Iago takes the opportunity to make Montano think that Cassio is a hopeless alcoholic. This seems to be confirmed when Cassio reappears threatening to beat Roderigo *into a twiggen bottle* (so that the weals on his skin look like wicker-work). Montano attempts to restrain Cassio and is attacked for his pains. Othello, presumably aroused from his marriage bed, angrily threatens the brawlers and appeals to Iago for an explanation. Montano pleads self-defence, and Iago cleverly defends Cassio so unconvincingly that Othello assumes he does so out of a desire to conceal Cassio's guilt.

'NEVER MORE BE OFFICER OF MINE'

Firm but fair – if somewhat credulous – Othello pronounces sentence: *Cassio, I love thee/ But never more be officer of mine*. Notice that Desdemona enters before he speaks the second line. Thus when pleading Cassio's case later she must know that she is trying to make Othello go back on a pledge made in public. ✪ How might this affect Othello's reputation?

Having secured Cassio's dismissal, Iago now presents himself as his sympathetic friend, giving him the same kind of manly advice that he gave the lovesick Roderigo. Reputation, he says *is an idle and most false imposition, oft got without merit and lost without deserving*. Ironically, the first part of this applies to him. Cassio is pessimistic, but Iago, weaving his web of deceit, reassures him: get Desdemona to plead his case, and Othello will have him back. Cassio departs, cheered and grateful. ✪ How should the actor playing Cassio show this change?

COMMENTARY

'DIVINITY OF HELL!'

Alone again, Iago seems to challenge the audience: *And what's he then that says I play the villain?* The soliloquy falls into two parts. First he pretends to be defending himself, saying that his advice is free and *honest* (echoing all the characters who describe him as such). He points out that Desdemona is generous-hearted and Othello is a slave to her wishes, and that therefore it would indeed appear to be Cassio's best course to appeal to her. His reference to Desdemona's *appetite*, as before, suggests sexual desire. The phrase *parallel course* prepares us for the change of tone about to come. It means this advice will actually lead Cassio directly away from what he seeks.

Iago now drops the pretence of innocence completely with the explosive *Divinity of hell!* He compares himself to a deceitful devil, and to a murderer pouring *pestilence* into Othello's ear (as did Claudius to Hamlet's father in *Hamlet*). His mention of *blackest sins* and of turning Desdemona's *virtue into pitch* echoes the racist view that Othello's blackness makes him damned. The image of *the net/ That shall enmesh them all* suggests a trap set for animals.

57

There is a short exchange between Iago and Roderigo, in which the schemer reassures his gullible victim that the beating he received has been worthwhile. Finally, Iago unfolds the next stage of his plan: to get Desdemona to plead for Cassio, and to arrange things so that Othello will come across Cassio *jump* (the word is used adverbially) just when Cassio is *soliciting* Desdemona for help.

Act 2: test your knowledge and understanding

(Answers at end of Commentary, page 84)

1. What practical result does the storm have?
2. How does the storm relate to the mood of the play?
3. How does Desdemona explain her bantering with Iago?
4. Who describes whom as *a slipper and subtle knave*, and why is this ironic?
5. What are the *offices* declared open in scene 2?
6. What weakness in Cassio does Iago play on?
7. What three things does Cassio describe as *exquisite*?
8. What line expresses the finality of Othello's judgement on Cassio?
9. What does Iago intend to get Emilia to do, as the first step in his plan, and why?

Your views

1. How do we see Othello behave in this Act, and what does it show about him?
2. How far do you think Cassio deserves to lose his post, and why?
3. How does Iago see himself?

Cassio's taking a break. Time you did too.

COMMENTARY

Act 3, scene 1

- Cassio pays musicians to play outside Othello's window.
- The Clown, on Othello's behalf, pays the musicians to stop.
- Iago gets Emilia to arrange for Cassio to speak to Desdemona.

The Clown in *Othello* is not one of Shakespeare's best. His jokes are rather laboured. For example, his opening question is an obscene suggestion that the musicians have caught syphilis (thought to be common in Naples). This disease eventually eats away the sufferer's nose. Having a 'clown' (a low-class joker rather than a clown in the modern sense) baiting musicians was a standard theatrical 'comic turn'. However, this clown does have a dramatic purpose: to get rid of the musicians and to fetch Emilia for Cassio. He also provides light relief after the previous scene. Iago assures Cassio that he will arrange for him to speak to Desdemona when Othello is out of the way. Emilia, unaware of Iago's true purpose, offers Cassio hope and says she will *bestow* (place) him where he will be able to speak freely to Desdemona.

Act 3, scene 2

- Othello gives Iago instructions and supervises the fortifications of the island.

This brief scene shows two things: (1) Iago is becoming Othello's right-hand man in Cassio's absence; (2) Othello still has a working life in which Desdemona plays no part.

Act 3, scene 3

- Desdemona tells Cassio she will plead for his reinstatement.
- As Othello and Iago arrive, Cassio departs.
- Iago begins to plant suspicion in Othello's mind.
- Desdemona pleads Cassio's case.
- Desdemona drops her handkerchief, which Emilia finds and gives to Iago.
- Iago gives Othello further 'proof' of Desdemona's infidelity.

OTHELLO

◆ Othello vows revenge on Cassio and Desdemona, and Iago vows to help him.

'HIS BED SHALL SEEM A SCHOOL'

Desdemona assures Cassio that Othello is only putting off reinstating him because it would look bad to do so immediately. She says they will soon be friends again, rashly promising him his post back and saying she will not let Othello rest until this is achieved: *His bed shall seem a school, his board a shrift* (his table a place of confession). ✪ How do you view this promise, given that it may jeopardize her marriage?

COMMENTARY

When Othello and Iago enter, Cassio thinks he had better leave, so Iago is able to plant the first seed of jealousy with the line *Ha, I like not that.* He uses the same technique as he did after the brawl: he defends Cassio in such a way as to make him seem guilty. Desdemona plunges straight into her campaign, nagging her husband to name the time when he will meet Cassio. Insensitive to his response, she repeatedly urges him to name a time, pleads that Cassio's offence is slight and that he is penitent, and wonders that she should have to work so hard to get Othello to agree, when it is for his own good. Twice he says, *I will deny thee nothing,* the second time asking to be left alone – to which she agrees. ✪ How do you judge her insistence? And how do you think she and Othello should be played in this scene?

THE SEED OF SUSPICION

With Desdemona gone, Othello calls her *Excellent wretch,* and seems to exclaim that he loves her despite himself. For a moment he seems to sweep aside his suspicion. His assertion *when I love thee not/ Chaos is come again* refers to the Greek creation myth in which the universe begins in Chaos (the Void), and then gives birth to the god of love, Eros. The lines may also foreshadow the chaos (perhaps in the more modern sense of disorder) that is to descend on Othello's mind.

Iago plants further suspicion by an apparently innocent question, and then deliberately says very little, implying that he is holding something back too terrible to mention. Notice how he merely echoes Othello's questions rather than answer them properly, so that Othello begins to imagine *some monster in thy thought/ Too hideous to be shown.* Such is Othello's trust in Iago that he even says that in *a false disloyal knave* this might be trickery, but not in Iago! Iago further winds up Othello's anxieties by insisting on his right to keep his thoughts to himself – since, after all, they may be *vile and false.* Then he insists that it will be better for Othello not to know them, and talks vaguely of reputation. When he warns Othello against *the green-eyed monster, which doth mock/ The meat it feeds on,* he is still saying, in effect, 'Don't listen to me.' This, naturally, has the opposite effect to the one at which it pretends to aim.

Although shaken, Othello insists that he will not be jealous without proof: after all, Desdemona chose him. However, if he once has proof, that will be the end of his love. Iago, ever the opportunist, now changes tack, pretending that Othello's show of sound judgement has persuaded him that it is safe to be more frank. He tells Othello, *Look to your wife, observe her well with Cassio*, says that Venetian women cannot be trusted, and points out that Desdemona deceived her father. Othello tries to persuade himself, and Iago, that he is unaffected: *Not a jot, not a jot ... No, not much moved.* He insists, unconvincingly, that Desdemona is *honest*, and Iago needles his doubts again with a typical pretence at

reassurance: *long live you to think so.* The moment Othello falters, Iago has the audacity to try another argument: namely, that the very fact of her marrying Othello, rather than someone *Of her own clime, complexion and degree* suggests that she is unnatural and perverted.

Iago suggests that Othello should put off reinstating Cassio. If Desdemona pleads for him, this will suggest her guilt. He exits, leaving Othello to torture himself in the soliloquy beginning *This fellow's of exceeding honesty.* We see how disturbed Othello is by the rapidity with which he proceeds from *If I do prove her haggard* (like an untameable hawk), to *Haply for I am black* (considering reasons for her preferring Cassio), then to the sudden conclusion: *She's gone, I am abused, and my relief/ Must be to loathe her.* Notice how his imagery now turns to disgust, imprisonment and disease:

> *I had rather be a toad*
> *And live upon the vapour of a dungeon*
> *Than keep a corner in the thing I love*
> *For others' uses. Yet 'tis the plague of great ones ...*

THE HANDKERCHIEF IS LOST AND FOUND

Despite the effect that Iago has already had on Othello, when Desdemona enters, Othello shows that he is not quite convinced: *I'll not believe't.* He may genuinely have a headache, as he claims, but we may imagine him placing his thumb and forefinger on his forehead where a cuckold's horns might grow. It is in trying to comfort him that Desdemona drops her handkerchief, which is then found by Emilia. Although Emilia does not know Iago's plan, she is guilty in that she deceives Desdemona by taking it. (Her guilt deepens in the next scene.)

In the exchange between Iago and Emilia we see his scorn for her. Her stealing of the handkerchief seems a pathetic attempt to please him. Iago again shows his gift for improvisation, privately deciding to plant the handkerchief in Cassio's lodging, where Cassio will find it. We see Iago's methods again in the line *This may do something*. In other words, he has a vague idea of how to use the handkerchief, but has not as yet worked out his plan in detail.

IGNORANCE WAS BLISS

When Iago sees Othello coming, he speaks some of the most beautiful lines in the play:

Look where he comes. Not poppy nor mandragora
Nor all the drowsy syrups of the world
Shall ever medicine thee to that sweet sleep
Which thou owedst yesterday.

This poignantly voices the bitter fact that Othello cannot turn back the clock to a time when his 'ignorance' was bliss. Speak the lines aloud. Notice how the first line breaks from the rhythm of iambic pentameter, forcing you to slow down on 'mandragora' (mandrake). The **alliteration** (poetic repetition of consonant sounds) of the sliding 's' sounds and soft 'th' sounds in the last three lines adds to this effect, as well as sounding sleepy. Although it appears that Othello does not hear this speech, he takes up the theme himself. He was happy while he had no *sense ... of her stolen hours of lust*. Othello further tortures himself with this idea:

I had been happy if the general camp,
Pioneers and all, had tasted her sweet body,
So I had nothing known.

Pioneers were the lowest kind of soldier in the camp. The image of them 'tasting' her *sweet body* taps into Othello's sensuality (see Commentary for Act 4, scene 2). This mention of soldiers gives way to a set-piece 'farewell to glory' speech,

OTHELLO

a popular literary convention. Othello is saying that he is a broken man, no longer capable of sustaining his career. Notice the rather melodramatic repetition of *farewell*. Count how many times it appears in the speech. ○ How do you regard this speech? Is it simply true? Is Othello dramatizing himself again?

OTHELLO DEMANDS PROOF
(Also see essay, page 101)

With the changeability now characteristic of his increasingly unbalanced mind, Othello now seizes Iago and threatens him: *Villain, be sure thou prove my love a whore,/ Be sure of it, give me the ocular proof.* This enables Iago to protest against his honesty being repaid with violence. Moreover, Othello's demand for *ocular proof* gives Iago a new idea: he will goad Othello further by dwelling on this idea of him catching the lovers in the act of adultery. In the suggestive speech beginning *It were a tedious difficulty, I think ...*, he uses animal imagery to paint a picture of the 'lovers' in their lust. In speaking of circumstantial evidence leading *directly to the door of truth*, he leads Othello, in his inflamed imagination, right to the bedroom door behind which Desdemona and Cassio are making love. His false report of Cassio's 'dream' adds to the impression, all the more so when Iago pretends to dismiss it as evidence: *Nay, this was but his dream.*

When Iago reports, as further 'evidence' that he saw Cassio wipe his beard with Desdemona's handkerchief, Othello is incensed. The picture suggests not only that Desdemona has given him the handkerchief as a love token, but that Cassio treats her love lightly. Othello speaks increasingly of revenge, wishing that Cassio had *forty thousand lives* for him to take. In what is perhaps meant to suggest magical (and therefore pagan African) ritual, Othello acts out 'blowing' his love, like dust, back to heaven.

The remainder of this speech, from *Arise, black vengeance*, is an appeal to dark powers, like Lady Macbeth's speech beginning *Come, you spirits/ That tend on mortal thoughts* (*Macbeth*, Act 1, scene 5). And rather like Macbeth picturing his mind full of scorpions, Othello pictures

COMMENTARY

his heart full of *aspics* – venomous snakes. He also compares his will with the *Pontic sea*, which was thought to flow only in one direction. He kneels and solemnly vows revenge, to which Iago adds his own vow to help him. Iago promises to kill Cassio, and Othello tells him: *Now art thou my lieutenant.*
✪ Do you take this as a formal promotion, or is Othello referring only to the campaign of revenge?

Act 3, scene 4

- Desdemona and Emilia come looking for Cassio and are met by the Clown.
- Othello asks for Desdemona's handkerchief and explains how special it is.
- Desdemona denies losing the handkerchief and Othello angrily exits.
- Desdemona tells Cassio she will do her best to get him reinstated.
- Emilia suggests that Othello may be jealous.
- Cassio meets Bianca and asks her to copy the pattern of the handkerchief.

CLOWNING AROUND

Desdemona seeks Cassio, perhaps to report her lack of progress in restoring his favour. She is met by the Clown in a short episode often omitted in productions. The Clown amuses himself with the usual puns, but Desdemona is in no mood to join in. ✪ Why do you think Shakespeare included this episode? Does it provide light relief or just hold up the plot?

'THE HANDKERCHIEF!'

Desdemona is worried about the handkerchief. Yet ironically she thinks that Othello is too noble to be made jealous: *the sun where he was born/ Drew all such humours from him.* This suggests the stereotype of the happy, trusting African. How little she knows him! When Othello himself arrives, she is determined to press him to take Cassio back. He pretends to read her palm, detecting *fruitfulness and liberal heart*, which is deliberately ambiguous. ✪ Is he playing with her, or is he still unsure of her guilt?

65

Desdemona pleads for Cassio, but Othello asks for her handkerchief, on the pretence of needing it to wipe his eye. He impresses on her that it has supernatural powers, and that for her to lose it or give it away would bring serious consequences. A prophetess who had predicted the end of the world sewed it in an inspired frenzy, its silk came from sanctified silkworms, and it was dyed in medicinal fluid made from embalmed corpses. Desdemona is shocked into a white lie: *It is not lost.* ⊙ How far is she to blame here? The couple become locked into opposing aims – he to see the handkerchief, she to argue Cassio's case. The conflict of misunderstanding rises to a pitch of tension, and Othello exits with *Zounds!* (God's wounds).

Emilia could now own up to her theft, but instead she warns Desdemona that Othello is jealous, and then complains about men in general: *They are all but stomachs, and we all but food.* Iago and Cassio now enter, Iago insisting that only Desdemona can help him. She asks Cassio to be patient: she will do what she can, but at present *My lord is not my lord* (he is not himself). Iago takes the opportunity to increase her anxiety, saying that for such a self-possessed man to be angry there must be something seriously wrong. Desdemona is quick to excuse Othello, hoping that he has only been put out by affairs of state. Emilia again worries about him being jealous.

'SWEET BIANCA'

The scene ends with an encounter between Cassio and Bianca. She is not a high-ranking woman, and she is pursuing him. Yet she is not necessarily a prostitute as sometimes portrayed. Notice how she has counted the hours since she last saw him. He apologizes and calls her *Sweet Bianca*, then asks her to copy the needlework of the handkerchief, which he has found in his room (left there by Iago). She is immediately jealous, thinking it comes from a rival. His response to her *vile guesses* is hardly conciliatory.

COMMENTARY

Act 3: test your knowledge and understanding

(Answers at end of Commentary, page 85)

1. Who says *Ha, I like not that,* and to what does it refer?
2. Desdemona urges Othello to name a time. For what?
3. Why does Iago echo Othello's questions rather than answering properly?
4. What is *the green-eyed monster*?
5. How does Iago argue that Desdemona must be unnatural?
6. Of what does Othello demand *ocular proof*, and from whom?
7. What vows do Othello and Iago make?
8. What white lie does Desdemona tell, and why?
8. What makes Bianca jealous?

Your views

1. How easily, in your opinion, is Othello persuaded by Iago?
2. How far do you think Desdemona is to blame for Othello's mounting jealousy?
3. Should Bianca be portrayed sympathetically? And what does Cassio's casual attitude towards her reveal?

Hopefully you won't need mandragora to unwind. Take a break!

Act 4, scene 1

- Iago stirs Othello's jealousy to such a pitch that he has a fit.
- Othello thinks Iago and Cassio are discussing Desdemona.
- Othello decides to strangle Desdemona.
- He strikes her in front of Lodovico.

OTHELLO HAS A FIT

The scene opening suggests that Iago and Othello have been talking for some time. Othello at first seems distracted, echoing Iago in a reversal of their roles in Act 3, scene 3. Iago is suggesting what a woman, or Desdemona in particular, might do in apparent innocence – knowing full well that Othello will not take it as such. Seeing that Othello is sufficiently aroused, Iago slips into his mind the idea of the handkerchief, which casts a shadow over Othello's mind *As doth the raven o'er the infectious house.* The raven, as in *Macbeth*, is a bad omen, especially appearing over a plague-infected household.

Iago continues to play Othello like a fish, feigning reluctance to incriminate either Desdemona or Cassio. The idea of the handkerchief, coupled with Cassio lying with, or on, Desdemona, is too much for Othello. Notice how his language becomes disjointed, signifying that his mind is falling apart: *Pish! Noses, ears and lips. Is't possible? Confess! handkerchief! O devil!* He falls into a *trance*, or a fit, and Iago enjoys the spectacle of Othello's helplessness for a few moments before raising the alarm. Notice Iago's use of the word *medicine* to describe what he is doing to Othello. (Compare this with its use earlier; see Commentary for Act 3, scene 3.) Iago tells Cassio that this is Othello's second fit in two days. This will help to undermine Othello's reputation for reliability. When Othello revives, Iago confirms that he is a cuckold, but adds that he is one of many. ❂ Do you think Iago genuinely believes that so many women are unfaithful?

'OCULAR PROOF'

Iago tells Othello to hide and watch while he gets Cassio to describe his affair with Desdemona. With

COMMENTARY

Othello out of the way, we hear that Iago plans to get Cassio talking about Bianca. He quickly does so, lowering his voice as he speaks her name, so that Othello will construe the conversation as being about Desdemona. We cannot be sure whether Othello hears every word, or just gets the gist, helped by Cassio's laughter, gestures and facial expressions. If Othello does hear it all, Iago is lucky that Cassio doesn't give the game away. (He almost does when he calls himself Bianca's *customer*.) At any rate, Othello is now so far gone that he would take Cassio's laughter alone as evidence. The laughter confirms the 'evidence' that Iago produced earlier, of Cassio supposedly wiping his beard with Desdemona's handkerchief. Both details argue that Cassio treats his affair with Desdemona lightly. When Bianca herself appears, Cassio is offhand with her. He refers to her as a *fitchew* (polecat). Though angry about the handkerchief, she invites him to dinner. ✪ What is your attitude towards them both now?

Othello swings between desire for revenge, both on Cassio and Desdemona, disgust, and sorrow for what he thinks he has lost. He declares that his heart has turned to stone, yet the next moment he is proclaiming, *O, the world hath not a sweeter creature*. Again, his plaintive repetition of *the pity of it* gives way to the savage *I will chop her into messes!* In this turmoil he tells Iago to get him some poison. Iago, however, probably fearing that this will implicate him in the murder, suggests that it will be more fitting to *strangle her in her bed – even the bed she hath contaminated*. And so the tragic end draws one step nearer.

OTHELLO STRIKES DESDEMONA

Othello's downfall now begins to be made public. As he reads a letter from Venice, Desdemona, still doing her best for Cassio, tells the message bearer, Lodovico, that she would do much to reconcile Othello and Cassio, *for the love I bear to Cassio*. This enrages Othello, who strikes the confused Desdemona, to the amazement of Lodovico. Othello's disjointed speech beginning *Ay, you did wish that I would make her turn ...* hints at Desdemona's supposed infidelity but makes little sense to Lodovico. Its ending, *Goats and monkeys!*, echoes Iago's description of the lecherous lovemaking between Desdemona and Cassio, but it must seem

OTHELLO

odd to Lodovico. No wonder that he doubts Othello's fitness to serve the state. Iago encourages these doubts.

Act 4, scene 2

- ◆ Othello questions Emilia about Desdemona.
- ◆ He summons Desdemona and accuses her of falsehood.
- ◆ Emilia and Iago sympathize with Desdemona.
- ◆ Emilia suspects that someone has slandered Desdemona.
- ◆ Roderigo suspects that Iago is duping him.

OTHELLO'S DISGUST

The scene at first holds out some hope for Desdemona. Othello questions Emilia, who has seen nothing to suggest that she is unfaithful. Othello says *That's strange*, but still accuses Desdemona of being *false as hell*. In the fine speech beginning *Had it pleased heaven ...*, he says that he could have found patience to bear sores, shame, poverty and

COMMENTARY

captivity, and even the scorn to which he must now be subjected. However, he cannot bear the corruption of Desdemona, in whom he had placed all his hopes, and on whom his life depends:

> *But there where I have garnered up my heart,*
> *Where either I must live or bear no life,*
> *The fountain from the which my current runs*
> *Or else dries up – to be discarded thence!*
> *Or keep it as a cistern for foul toads*
> *To knot and gender in!*

As in Act 3, scene 3, we find an image of toads, this time seen mating. This expresses Othello's sense of disgust and revulsion at finding the wellspring of his life apparently polluted.

Critics have commented on Othello's extreme sensuality, and we see it when he switches from the gross image of flies in the meat market (*shambles*) to Desdemona as a *weed* [masquerading as a flower]/ *Who art so lovely fair and smell'st so sweet/ That the sense aches at thee*. He paints a picture of heaven, the moon and even *the bawdy wind*, all unable to bear the awfulness of her crime. As the scene borders on violence, he calls her *that cunning whore of Venice*, and gives money to Emilia, saying *We have done our course*, as if Desdemona is indeed a whore and he is a satisfied customer. After he leaves, Desdemona is so shocked that she cannot even weep.

IAGO ON THE DEFENSIVE

When Iago enters, he feigns disbelief that Othello could so abuse Desdemona. However, in a rush of insight Emilia comes dangerously close to the truth: that *some eternal villain ... to get some office* has *devised this slander*. The heartfelt way in which she describes the villain makes us wonder if she suspects Iago. Certainly, he senses danger, which is why he dismisses her theory: *Fie, there's no such man, it is impossible.* Undaunted, Emilia continues, even praying that such villains might be whipped naked through the world, so that Iago nervously cautions her: *Speak within doors* (either less loudly or more guardedly). She comes even closer to the truth when she recalls Iago once suspecting that she had been unfaithful with Othello. Desdemona, still too shocked to notice the drift of the conversation, vows her love for Othello. Iago weakly reassures her.

With the women gone, Iago tackles another problem: Roderigo, not completely stupid, is beginning to realize he has been duped by Iago. He complains: *The jewels you have had from me to deliver to Desdemona would have corrupted a votarist* [someone who has made religious vows, especially of celibacy]. Iago is at first brief and non-committal, perhaps considering his options: *Well, go to; very well ... Very well ... You have said now*. Then he has an idea. He congratulates Roderigo on his *mettle* and tells him that Othello has been summoned to Mauretania: the only way to prevent him – and Desdemona – going is to kill Cassio, so that there is no one to replace Othello. Iago is 'thinking on his feet' and Roderigo is not quite convinced. However, the ploy takes the immediate pressure off Iago. ❂ How safe is he now?

Act 4, scene 3

- ◆ Othello walks with Lodovico and Desdemona, then sends Desdemona to bed.
- ◆ Desdemona prepares for bed, singing sadly and talking with Emilia.

This scene adds nothing to the plot of the play but is essential to the development of its mood, and in preparing us for Desdemona's death. It is also remarkable for its 'feminist' sentiments.

Othello and Lodovico walk together, with Desdemona and Emilia. When Othello sends Desdemona to bed, she meekly obeys. The quiet exchange between her and Emilia which now takes place is a calm before the storm (like the sad but peaceful scene in *Macbeth* before Lady Macduff and her children are murdered). When Emilia wishes that Desdemona had never seen Othello, Desdemona only reaffirms her love for him, with all his faults. For the tragedy to be effective we must believe wholly in Desdemona's goodness, and this is a reminder of it. We must also be prepared for her death. This is

COMMENTARY

achieved by what seems to be Desdemona's premonition: *If I do die before thee, prithee shroud me/ In one of these same sheets.* If you have studied *Romeo and Juliet*, you may recall similar moments in which both Romeo and Juliet have misgivings about what is to come.

Emilia tries to cheer Desdemona up: *Come, come, you talk.* When Desdemona recollects the sad story of her mother's maid, Barbary, Emilia tries to distract her by saying what a handsome man Lodovico is. Note that although A.J. Honigmann gives the line to Emilia in the Arden edition, some editors (including Kenneth Muir in the New Penguin edition) give it to Desdemona. This would suggest that she is wishing that she had married Lodovico instead of Othello. At any rate, Desdemona does not follow up this idea, instead singing the mournful 'Willow' song that Barbary sang at her death. (The willow symbolizes grief, especially for love.)

Desdemona asks Emilia if she thinks there really are women who betray their husbands. More worldly-wise than her mistress, Emilia says there are, and that she might do so herself if offered *all the whole world.* This leads on to her striking 'feminist' speech, reminiscent of Shylock's *Hath not a Jew ...* speech in *The Merchant of Venice.* Whereas Shylock says that Jews are as human as gentiles, Emilia says that women have resentments, desires and needs, just as men do. She insists that if women *fall* (into infidelity) it is the fault of their husbands, and that if men *slack their duties* (especially in bed), are unfaithful, jealous, restrictive, violent or mean, women have cause for revenge. In short, men had better treat them well: *... else let them know,/ The wills we do, their ills instruct us so.*

Act 4: test your knowledge and understanding

(Answers at end of Commentary, page 85)

1. What comes over Othello's memory *As doth the raven o'er the infectious house*?
2. How does Othello misinterpret a conversation between Iago and Cassio?
3. What shocks Lodovico, and why?

OTHELLO

4 Why does Othello tell Emilia *We have done our course*?
5 Who does Emilia think should be whipped naked through the world?
6 What does Roderigo claim *would have corrupted a votarist*?
7 What suggests that Desdemona anticipates her death?
8 What does the willow symbolize in Desdemona's song?
9 What does Emilia claim in her 'feminist' speech to Desdemona?

Your views

1 What do you feel about the trick Iago plays on Othello in getting him to witness the conversation? How far are Othello and Cassio to blame?
2 What do you make of Emilia's 'feminist' speech? Was Shakespeare a feminist ahead of his time? What do you suppose his audiences made of it?

The tension's mounting. Take a break before violence erupts.

Act 5, scene 1

- Roderigo lies in wait for Cassio and attacks him, but Cassio wounds him.
- Iago wounds Cassio from behind.
- Othello gloats over Cassio.
- Lodovico and Gratiano arrive but are afraid to help.
- Iago appears, stabs Roderigo and bandages Cassio.
- Bianca appears and Iago tries to implicate her in the attack.

From this point the action moves swiftly to its conclusion, though not without further complications. The scene begins with a rhyming couplet. These are more often found at the end of a scene. Here it may suggest the neat conclusion

COMMENTARY

that Iago would like to see – Cassio dead, or perhaps even Cassio and Roderigo killed by each other, which would suit him even better. Roderigo is anxious about killing Cassio, and fears both failure and success. He asks Iago to stay close by, yet he has to persuade himself that if Cassio dies *'Tis but a man gone.*

We see again how Iago pushes the action in a general direction while preparing to make the most of whatever occurs: *Every way makes my gain.* If Roderigo lives, he may still demand the gold and jewels that Iago has got out of him supposedly to give to Desdemona. If Cassio lives, there is a chance that Othello will challenge him and find out that Iago has been lying. The other reason Iago now gives for wanting Cassio dead is stranger: *He hath a daily beauty in his life/ That makes me ugly.* This is rather like Macbeth's comment on Banquo: ... *under him/ My genius is rebuk'd* (*Macbeth*, Act 3, scene 3). ✪ How do you interpret Iago's line? Is he envious? Does he feel inferior?

Roderigo's thrust at Cassio is deflected by Cassio's mail undercoat, which is why Iago targets his unprotected legs. Othello, coming across Cassio wounded, assumes that Iago has killed him as he promised. This fires him with resolution to kill Desdemona, whom he contemptuously calls *Minion*. He talks about her bed being spotted with *lust's blood*, which creates a vivid picture in the mind's eye, although critics have noted that either Shakespeare or Othello must be unsure how to kill Desdemona, since in Act 4, scene 1 Othello said he would strangle her. Note that in the darkness Othello cannot see that Cassio is not mortally wounded.

Othello exits and is replaced on stage by Lodovico and Gratiano (Desdemona's uncle), who are afraid to help in case the groaning men are part of an ambush. This adds to the mood of distrust: even good deeds may lead to treachery. Iago comes *in his shirt, with light and weapons*, as if awoken from bed. Improvising as he often does, he stabs Roderigo, ridding himself of a liability and ensuring his silence. He has the excuse that Roderigo must have attacked Cassio, and no one questions this 'rough justice'. To shift possible blame farther from himself, he seizes the opportunity to blame the unfortunate Bianca, who is distraught to see Cassio injured.

OTHELLO

○ How do you interpret Iago's 'shocked' announcement that Cassio's attacker was his own friend and countryman Roderigo? Would he not be safer to deny knowing him?

Iago's ploy of throwing suspicion on Bianca – *I do suspect this trash* – is nasty, but likely to work, given Bianca's reputation. Even Emilia believes that the murder attempt represents *the fruits of whoring*. Bianca makes no attempt to deny that Cassio had supper with her, and it seems particularly unfair that Emilia abuses her: *O fie upon thee, strumpet!* ○ How do you judge Bianca, and Emilia's view of her?

The scene ends with Iago's observation, presumably heard only by the audience, that *This is the night/ That either makes me or fordoes me quite.* He knows he is playing a dangerous game. The tension is mounting.

Act 5, scene 2

- Othello accuses Desdemona and suffocates her.
- Desdemona revives momentarily.
- Emilia condemns Othello.
- Montano and Gratiano confront Othello.
- Emilia reveals Iago's trickery.
- Iago kills Emilia and escapes.
- Montano and Gratiano pursue Iago.
- Othello wounds Iago.
- Othello kills himself.
- Cassio is made governor of Cyprus.

DESDEMONA MURDERED

This final scene opens with Othello standing over his sleeping wife. (She has got to sleep very quickly, in the circumstances!) He is apparently persuading himself that he must indeed kill Desdemona. Three times he asserts *It is the cause*, though without stating what that cause is. It may simply be Desdemona's supposed infidelity, or it may be something more specific, such as the fact that *else she'll betray more men*, as he argues a few lines later. This rather unconvincing reasoning – as if he might let her live if she promised not to betray anyone else – merely shows that Othello is losing his grip.

COMMENTARY

🪶 The fact that Desdemona is sleeping does allow Othello to speak what in effect is a soliloquy. He regretfully admires her beauty, and then contemplates putting out the light of the candle, and then the light of her life – which cannot so easily be restored as that of the candle. He mentions Prometheus, who in Greek myth stole fire from the gods for mankind. We see Othello's sensuality even here, as he is about to kill Desdemona. He compares her to an unplucked rose, which he must smell while he can. Her *balmy breath* almost makes him go back on what he has now convinced himself is an act of justice.

🗣 The next part of the scene is controversial, since Desdemona is remarkably passive, making no attempt to escape, and little attempt to defend herself with words. When she awakes, Othello tells her to make her confession, since he would not kill her *unprepared spirit*. She is shocked but still speaks gently to him. When he finally accuses her of giving the handkerchief to Cassio, she denies it. Although Othello seems reluctant to mention the real crime of which he thinks her guilty, she begins to guess, and insists that she never loved Cassio except as a friend. He wants her to confess, to confirm that he is about to commit a noble sacrifice, not a murder. He is of course lying when he says that Cassio has confessed, unless he is referring to Cassio's conversation with Iago about Bianca. ✪ Given that Othello sees himself as noble, why does he lie at this point?

Hardly anything is spelled out between Othello and Desdemona. Othello seems to be obsessed with the handkerchief, and takes some time to spit out his real accusation: *That he hath – ud's death! – used thee.* Even now, his meaning is obscure, and Desdemona has to seek clarification: *How? unlawfully?* Desdemona's perfectly understandable grief for Cassio's death is taken by Othello as further proof of her guilt. But then even her line *Alas, he is betrayed, and I undone* is ambiguous. This could be taken to mean that someone has given away the secret of their affair. Desdemona pleads to be allowed to live a little longer, but Othello smothers her, even as she cries out to him as her *Lord*.

The tense stillness after Othello has smothered Desdemona is broken by Emilia outside the door. Othello's language betrays his uncertainty. It comes in short bursts, full of questions:

> *The noise was high. Ha, no more moving?*
> *Still as the grave. Shall she come in? were't good?*
> *I think she stirs again. No – what's best to do?*

And the awful finality of his deed begins to dawn on him. He feels as if nature itself should reflect what has happened, that there should be *a huge eclipse/ Of sun and moon.* (Early critic Thomas Rymer pointed out that this is impossible!) Still in

COMMENTARY

shock himself, when Emilia announces that murders have been done, he seems confused: *What? now?* He blames it on the moon, whom he refers to as *She*. Nonetheless he has the presence of mind to regret that Cassio is not dead: *Then murder's out of tune.*

Desdemona's revival, several minutes after being smothered, presents a problem to the modern mind (though it could be argued that modern film audiences suspend their disbelief when the knife-wielding psychopath revives in a similar style!). Medically speaking it is impossible: if someone who has apparently been suffocated revives enough to speak, they've recovered. However, probability aside, it allows Desdemona to declare her innocence to a third party – Emilia, and it allows her last words to be an act of loving self-sacrifice, risking damnation by protecting Othello. ❂ How would the scene be different without Desdemona's revival? Would it be better?

EMILIA CONDEMNS OTHELLO

Emilia fiercely defends her mistress and condemns Othello: *thou art a devil*. She is taken aback when she hears that Othello's informant is none other than her own husband. Three times she questions, in disbelief and growing understanding: *My husband?* In the end, Othello becomes exasperated: *I say thy husband: dost understand the word?* This finally provokes Emilia to burst out with a fierce denial, characteristically punitive (remember that in Act 4, scene 2 she wanted villains to be whipped naked round the world):

> *If he say so, may his pernicious soul*
> *Rot half a grain a day! he lies to th' heart:*
> *She was too fond of her most filthy bargain!*

Despite the racist jibe (the *bargain* is Othello), we must admire Emilia's nerve in so passionately confronting a man who is her master, the governor of Cyprus – and armed. When he threatens her she is undaunted and cries out that he has killed her mistress. Montano and Iago rush in, and Emilia desperately confronts her husband, hoping against hope that he is not the villain she thinks he is. He admits to telling Othello that Desdemona was false. Montano's condemnation of Othello gives Emilia the cue for another outburst, as her conviction that her husband is to blame grows to fever-pitch:

Villainy, villainy, villainy!
I think upon't, I think I smell't, O villainy!
I thought so then: I'll kill myself for grief!

She cannot bear to realize now that she suspected her husband, albeit vaguely, and failed to realize the truth. Iago now begins to worry that she will reveal all. Othello falls on the bed, beginning to doubt what he has done, although he still insists that what he did was right: *O, she was foul/ ... I know this act shows horrible and grim.* When Othello declares his 'evidence' – Cassio's 'confession' and his possession of the handkerchief, Emilia's worst fears are confirmed, and Iago becomes seriously worried. When she refuses to leave, he tries to stab her, but is presumably prevented from doing so by Gratiano. This intervention allows her to reveal that she gave the handkerchief to Iago.

THE GAME IS UP

The scene rises to a violent climax as Iago abuses his wife and accuses her of lying, Othello, realizing he has been tricked, lunges at Iago, and Iago stabs Emilia, then escapes. Notice the sequence. (The stage direction is unusually precise.) Iago must realize that if Othello is trying to kill him, the game is up. Therefore his motive for stabbing Emilia is probably furious revenge rather than any continued hope of maintaining his innocence. Certainly, Montano now has no doubts, declaring Iago *a notorious villain*. Think what a remarkable turnaround this is, for a character who has persistently been praised by everyone else as honest.

Montano and Gratiano exit in pursuit of Iago, and Emilia is left with Othello. Poignantly, Emilia sings a snatch of the 'Willow' song before finally reiterating Desdemona's innocence and devotion to Othello, then dying. Othello, now alone in the chamber, declares that he has another weapon. (Presumably Montano has taken the sword with which he tried to kill Iago.) Gratiano, outside, does not believe him, and enters. Othello now seems to take refuge in memories of his former glories, remembering how he once fought with this

COMMENTARY

same sword. Gratiano must look afraid (after all, he is elderly), but Othello tells him he has nothing to fear: *Here is my journey's end, here is my butt/ And very sea-mark of my utmost sail.* To paraphrase Othello's maritime metaphor, it is 'the end of the line' for him, so Gratiano need not worry.

Then Othello's eyes fall on Desdemona and once again he is pierced by regret, as he imagines how at Judgement Day, the look on her face will hurl him to damnation. Such is the bitterness of his remorse that he welcomes the tortures of hell. We are perhaps to imagine that, given his present anguish and sense of guilt, to be whipped by devils and roasted in sulphur will almost be a comfort to him. The speech ends in a cry from the wilderness: *O Desdemon! dead, Desdemon. Dead! O, O!*

When Iago is brought back in, together with the wounded Cassio in a chair, we embark on the last part of the scene, and of the play. Othello tries again to kill the *devil* Iago, but succeeds only in wounding him. Lodovico voices his pity for Othello, and Othello asks for Cassio's pardon. Iago, for his part, determines stubbornly never to speak again. ✪ What do you think is the dramatic effect of this?

OTHELLO'S SUICIDE

Now loose ends are tied up. Lodovico produces letters found on Roderigo that explain Iago's plot to those present. Cassio explains how he came to have Desdemona's handkerchief. Lodovico rules that Cassio (presumably expected to recover) will take over Othello's command, and that Iago is to be cunningly tortured. It seems as if the play might end here, but it is after all the tragedy of Othello, and so it now leads into his death speech. This is one of the most beautiful and dignified speeches in the play, indeed in Shakespeare. Othello in effect writes his own epitaph:

Speak of me as I am. Nothing extenuate,
Nor set down aught in malice. Then must you speak
Of one that loved not wisely, but too well;
Of one not easily jealous, but, being wrought,
Perplexed in the extreme.

Notice the stately rhythm, revealing that Othello has finally undergone a transformation. In the awful

OTHELLO

realization of his guilt, he has regained his presence of mind. In this play full of lies and deception, he now appeals for simple truth. ◯ How accurate do you think he is in describing himself?

The speech switches deftly to its final twist in the phrase *And say besides* .... Othello, first and foremost a soldier, a man of action, must die as a soldier. Perhaps he steels himself for the blow he must strike by recalling his former deeds. Producing a concealed knife, he kills himself as he once did the *circumcised dog*, the Turk, thus in his dying breath reaffirming that he sees himself very much as a Christian and a loyal Venetian. It remains only for Lodovico to conclude the play, saying that Othello's fortune falls to his nearest surviving relative by marriage, Desdemona's uncle Gratiano, and that the new lord governor, Cassio, is to decide on Iago's punishment.

Act 5: test your knowledge and understanding

(Answers at end of Commentary, page 86)

1 What reasons does Iago have for wanting Roderigo dead?
2 What reasons does Iago have for wanting Cassio dead?
3 Why are Lodovico and Gratiano afraid to help Cassio and Roderigo, and how is this significant?
4 What is Iago's excuse for stabbing Roderigo?
5 On whom does Iago try to pin the blame for the attack on Cassio?
6 How does Othello see his murder of Desdemona when he commits it?
7 Who is the first person to condemn Othello for murdering Desdemona?
8 How does Othello see the murder when he realizes he has been tricked?
9 What memory does Othello use to help him commit suicide?

COMMENTARY

Your views

1 How much sympathy do you feel for Roderigo, and why?
2 How do you see Desdemona by the time she dies? Would you respect her more if she were less passive?
3 What is your view of Bianca, and how important do you think she is?
4 When Othello learns how he has been tricked, he wants revenge, but he sees himself as guilty, not as Iago's innocent victim. How important is this for the play as a tragedy?

Well done — you've reached the tragic end. Take a well-earned break.

Answers to 'test your knowledge and understanding' sections

ACT 1

1. The night-time setting helps to create an atmosphere of confusion and uncertainty.
2. Othello is at first referred to only as *the Moor* to emphasize that he is a social outsider.
3. Iago refers to Othello as *an old black ram*, meaning that Othello is a bad match for Desdemona, being too old as well as black, and that his feeling for her is mere animal lust. Iago may believe this, but he also wants to provoke Brabantio.
4. Brabantio accuses Othello of bewitching Desdemona, since he cannot believe she would freely choose to marry a Moor.
5. Othello's response shows that he is calm, self-confident and refined.
6. The Turks pretend to be sailing for Rhodes, not Cyprus. This trickery is echoed in Iago's.
7. Othello says he won Desdemona's love by telling his life-story.
8. Brabantio warns Othello that Desdemona may deceive her husband as she did him.
9. Iago resents the fact that Othello has made Cassio his lieutenant instead of him, and he suspects Othello of having sex with Emilia.

ACT 2

1. The storm sinks most of the Turkish fleet.
2. The weather foreshadows the emotional storm raised in Othello.
3. Desdemona says that she is putting a brave face on her anxiety about Othello.
4. Iago describes Cassio in this way; in fact the description is better suited to Iago himself.
5. Food and drink outlets.
6. Cassio gets drunk easily.
7. Cassio describes Desdemona, English drinkers and Iago's song as *exquisite*.

COMMENTARY

8 *Never more be officer of mine.*
9 Iago intends to get Emilia to ask Desdemona to plead for Cassio's reinstatement.

ACT 3

1 Iago says *Ha, I like not that*, referring to the way in which Cassio leaves Desdemona when he sees Othello coming.
2 Inviting Cassio to visit, with a view to reinstating him.
3 To make Othello think he is holding back painful incriminating information.
4 Jealousy.
5 Desdemona married someone of a different race and social group.
6 Othello demands *ocular* [visible] *proof* of Desdemona's adultery, from Iago.
7 Othello vows to kill Desdemona, Iago to help him.
8 Desdemona says that the handkerchief is not lost.
9 Bianca thinks that Cassio was given the handkerchief by another lover.

ACT 4

1 The handkerchief.
2 Othello sees (and possibly hears) Cassio laughing and talking in an offhand manner to Iago about a mistress. Othello assumes this is Desdemona; in fact it is Bianca.
3 Lodovico is shocked when Othello hits Desdemona, because she is an apparently innocent young woman and it argues that Othello is unfit for his command.
4 Othello is speaking as if they are in a brothel and he is Desdemona's client.
5 Slandering villains.
6 The jewels he has given Iago to give as presents to Desdemona.
7 Her idea that, should she die before Emilia, she wants to be shrouded in one of her wedding sheets.
8 Lost or unrequited love.
9 That women have resentments, desires and needs, just as men do; that if women are unfaithful it is the fault of their husbands; and that women mistreated by men have cause for revenge.

ACT 5

1. Roderigo may demand compensation for the gold and jewels he gave Iago to give to Desdemona.
2. Iago fears that, if Othello confronts Cassio, his deception may emerge. He also resents Cassio for being better, more fortunate or more refined than himself (*He hath a daily beauty in his life/ That makes me ugly*).
3. It is night, and they fear that the groaning men may be robbers feigning injury while their accomplices lie in wait. This adds to the mood of distrust.
4. Roderigo appears to be one of Cassio's attackers.
5. Bianca.
6. He sees it as a noble act of self-sacrifice that will save other men from his own fate.
7. Emilia.
8. As a terrible sin.
9. The memory of killing a Turk, an enemy of Venice.

CRITICAL APPROACHES

At levels beyond GCSE you need to be aware of the main critical approaches to texts. A huge amount of criticism has been written about *Othello*, and you will only have time to read a small proportion of it. However, reading the critics themselves, in addition to this summary, will make you more confident about referring to their arguments in your essays. Even if you don't refer to critics by name, reading them will help you to understand the main issues of interpretation in the play.

Reading critically

Once you understand the play's plot and language, you need to start considering possible interpretations. When you read a good critic's interpretation of *Othello* you may be immediately convinced. However, another critic may present a perfectly valid but contradictory interpretation, so do apply your own judgement to what you read. When you have understood the points being made, ask yourself if they are justified by the evidence of the play. Form your own opinions and be prepared to back them up.

THE MAIN ISSUES

Othello is a controversial play. Below is a list of issues that critics have discussed. Look out for them in the rest of this chapter, and in your reading of criticism. Even more important, try to develop your own views on them.

1. How is it significant that Othello is black?
2. How far is Othello to blame for the tragedy? In particular, is he a jealous man, or just a rather trusting one?
3. How much has Othello learned about himself by the end of the play? Is he more concerned with his self-image than with Desdemona's death?
4. Is Iago a psychologically realistic character, with real motives, or a devilish stage villain – or both?
5. If Iago has motives, what are they?

6 Is Desdemona entirely innocent, and is she believable, or a male fantasy?
7 Is the play as a whole satifsying? (For example, some critics would prefer it if Desdemona survived.)
8 How far does Shakespeare conform to, or challenge, Elizabethan prejudices?

Early views

The earliest surviving critique of *Othello* comes from the pen of Thomas Rymer, writing in 1693. Although often dismissed, Rymer is entertaining and refreshingly unburdened by preconceptions about Shakespeare's greatness. Moreover, he does make some points which have been echoed since by more respected critics. Much of the play he finds either unbelievable or exasperating. Othello ('the Jealous Booby') he finds too credulous, Iago too unnatural – since he has no reason to help kill Desdemona. Rymer cannot believe that Desdemona would not realize that Othello suspected her, and have sense enough not to keep nagging him about Cassio. He also thinks it unlikely that Desdemona would marry Othello, let alone submit so readily to being murdered by him. That someone of Othello's rank could abuse his wife as Othello does, calling her a whore, Rymer thinks 'is sure the most absurd Maggot that ever bred from any Poets addle Brain'.

As to the handkerchief, Rymer fails to see its symbolism, and thinks it absurd to give a trivial object such dramatic weight. He complains that for Shakespeare to kill off Desdemona is unjust, 'barbaric' and 'arbitrary', and that the play lacks moral instruction. He concludes that, 'the tragical part is clearly none other than a Bloody Farce, without salt or savour.'

In 1765 Samuel Johnson was more flattering. Unlike Rymer, he finds the characterization wonderfully lifelike. His only criticism is that the play would be better without Act 1. Johnson would prefer the play to begin in Cyprus, with the story to that point being related to us through the characters.
◐ How well do you think this would work?

Samuel Taylor Coleridge (early nineteenth century), set a trend for several later critics. First, he sees Othello as 'the very opposite to a jealous man: he was noble, generous, open-hearted; unsuspicious and unsuspecting; and who, even after the exhibition of the handkerchief as evidence of his wife's guilt, bursts out in her praise'. (Unfortunately this leads Coleridge to voice the racism of his time, saying that such a noble hero could not possibly be a negro.) Secondly, Coleridge comments on 'Iago's passionless character, all *will* and intellect', and on his devilish malice: 'the motive-hunting of motiveless malignity – how awful!' To Coleridge, Iago is simply looking for reasons to do the evil deeds to which he is attracted. Charles Lamb and William Hazlitt, Coleridge's contemporaries, agree that Iago has no real motive, as does the influential Victorian critic Swinburne.

More recent views
BRADLEY

The most influential of the early modern critics of *Othello* is A.C. Bradley. Try to read his two essays on the play in his book *Shakespearean Tragedy* (1904), since they have provided a starting-point for many later critics, some of whom have largely accepted his comments, while others – notably F.R. Leavis – have reacted to them with scorn.

Bradley assumes that Shakespeare can do no wrong, and that therefore everything in the play is as he intended it. Bradley also treats the characters as if they were real people, subjectable to psychological analysis. He sees Iago not only as psychologically believable, but as a brilliant creation on a level with Hamlet, and of equal dramatic stature within the play as Othello. He tends to follow Coleridge's tendency to idealize Othello, emphasizing his enduring nobility.

Bradley sees Othello as a man 'indisposed to jealousy' yet 'unusually open to deception, and, if once wrought to passion, likely to act with little reflection, with no delay, and in the most decisive manner conceivable'. Othello is an exotic, romantic figure, poetic but not introspective. An outward-looking soldier, both dignified and passionate, he makes decisions and acts on them quickly – unlike Hamlet or the early Macbeth. In defence of Othello's response to Iago's persuasion, Bradley argues that Othello is not alone in trusting him; Othello is newly married and cannot know Desdemona very well; he is imaginative, and Iago is very clever; and Othello doesn't begin to get properly jealous until 'evidence' has been produced, late in Act 3, scene 3. Even on the verge of murder, a sense of justice makes him question Emilia. In Bradley's view, by Act 5 Othello is transformed: 'He is to save Desdemona from herself, not in hate but in honour; in honour, and also in love. His anger has passed; a boundless sorrow has taken its place.' Desdemona, for Bradley, is completely innocent.

Bradley devotes the whole of his second essay to Iago. He emphasizes that only in his soliloquies can Iago be believed, and yet all the other characters trust him. Bradley even suggests that in a sense the play is Iago's tragedy, since opportunity tempts him to release his own destructive forces, which destroy him. He is cold rather than sadistic. He hates Othello, merely resents Cassio, despises Roderigo, and has no particular feeling at all for Desdemona. He gets pleasure from seeing his will worked out through his schemes, but he is not 'purely' evil. Rather, he is an artist, as Hazlitt says, 'an amateur of tragedy in real life', or in Swinburne's words 'an inarticulate poet'. He is compelled by a twisted creative urge. Honigmann, in his introduction to the Arden edition, also takes this view. The hunting for motives identified by Coleridge is, to Bradley, a sign that Iago has a conscience, while his comparison of himself with Cassio, who 'hath a daily beauty in his life' (Act 5, scene 1), suggests either that he sees himself as ugly (and therefore has a moral sense) or thinks that others see him as such (and is thus not a complete egoist). In short, Iago is a subtly portrayed human being, not a monster.

ELIOT AND LEAVIS

The poet T.S. Eliot took a rather different view of Othello's character in his 'Shakespeare and the Stoicism of Seneca' (1927). He sees Othello's suicide speech as an exposure of human weakness, not a testament to Othello's greatness: 'What Othello seems to me to be doing in making this speech is *cheering himself up*. He is endeavouring to escape reality, he has ceased to think about Desdemona, and is thinking about himself.'

F.R. Leavis, in his essay 'Diabolic Intellect and the Noble Hero' (1952) takes this criticism of Othello further. He complains that Bradley sees Othello as 'a nearly faultless hero whose strength and virtue are turned against him', whereas the truth is that Othello's character is largely to blame for the tragedy, and Iago is 'merely ancillary ... not much more than a necessary piece of dramatic mechanism'. For Leavis, Bradley makes the mistake of believing in Othello's own view of himself.

Leavis disagrees with Bradley on the question of how soon Othello begins to get jealous. Bradley thinks that the speech in which Othello decides *She's gone, I am abused, and my relief/ Must be to loathe her* (Act 3, scene 3) shows the first hint of jealousy; Leavis thinks that it is just the first outright statement of a jealousy that has long been brewing and that Iago simply plays on Othello's innate potential for jealousy.

Leavis acknowledges that Othello is 'the nobly massive man of action, the captain of men, he sees himself as being'. However, he thinks that Othello has a habit of 'self-approving self-dramatization', as shown when he explains how Desdemona fell in love with him (Act 1, scene 3) and in his 'farewell to glory' speech in Act 3, scene 3, lines 348–60. This self-image, says Leavis, serves Othello well enough as a military commander, but not as a husband. In fact Leavis questions whether Othello ever really loves Desdemona, claiming that his feelings for her are based on self-ignorance, self-centred pride, possessiveness, desire and love of loving. As evidence of this, and of the ugliness lurking beneath Othello's noble exterior, Leavis quotes such lines as *I will chop her into messes. Cuckold me!* (Act 4, scene 1). On the other hand, Leavis denies that Othello's poetry indicates that he is a natural poet; rather, it is simply Shakespeare's means of expression.

In Leavis' view, as Othello approaches the murder, he is preoccupied with his own emotions; his questioning of Emilia, and his ignoring her answers, shows injustice; when he realizes his mistake his reaction is to say, in effect, 'I could kick myself'; and his final speeches are full of self-pity and a desire for people to think well of him. ✪ How valid do you find Leavis' comments?

Of course, you need not agree entirely with either Bradley or Leavis. Christopher Norris, in 'Post-Structuralist Shakespeare', sees them both as bending the text to fit their own ideas. Whereas Bradley idealizes Othello, Leavis deflates him on the basis of his own preconceptions about poetry, and in particular his rejection of a 'sentimentality' which he assumes to be Othello's rather than Shakespeare's. Norris sees Bradley and Leavis as being influenced by the dynamics of the play, Bradley's approach reflecting the credulity of Othello, that of Leavis the cynicism of Iago.

Other critics, such as Kenneth Muir in his introduction to the Penguin New Shakespeare edition, have steered a middle course between Bradley and Leavis. Muir thinks that Shakespeare intends us to believe that Othello is not a jealous type. He is genuinely noble, but still deluded at the end of the play. He has a sense of occasion but is not melodramatic. He proclaims his own merits, but this would have been acceptable to the Elizabethans.

WILSON KNIGHT

G. Wilson Knight, in 'The *Othello* Music' (1930), approaches the play through its language. For him, the play's dominant quality is 'separation'. Its characteristic images stand alone in a way that is not true, say, of *Macbeth* or *King Lear*. He quotes as an example Othello's speech in which he compares his will to the one-way surge of the Pontic Sea (Act 3, scene 3). Individual words such as *mandragora* or *Anthropophagi* also stand out from the rest of the text in a similar way. Wilson Knight sees this as reflected in the separation of the characters, who fail to communicate or understand each other because they are completely different from each other.

Wilson Knight sees Othello's language as being, at first, poetically grand, exotically beautiful and dramatic. Later, as he is corrupted by Iago, it becomes ugly, revealing an ugliness of character beneath the nobility. Then at the end the nobility is restored, and we know that Othello's crime has been gullibility rather than anything worse. However, Wilson Knight does anticipate Leavis in seeing Othello as a sentimentalist, inclined to glorify himself. Iago, on the other hand, is essentially a cynic who loathes beauty. And, as Wilson Knight says, 'Logically, the cynic must oppose the sentimentalist.'

FEMINISM AND RACE

Some feminist critics have shifted the focus to Desdemona. Marilyn French, in *Shakespeare's Division of Experience*

CRITICAL APPROACHES

(1982) argues that Desdemona largely accepts her given role as an obedient wife, even to the extent of allowing her own murder. For French, Iago embodies the dominant values of a male-dominated world.

Karen Newman, in 'And Wash the Ethiop White', links the marginalization of women in the play to that of Othello as a black man, and agrees that Iago embodies male norms. She points out that the white pages of Desdemona's *goodly book* are blackened by having *whore* written across them (Act 4, scene 3, lines 72–3). One could add that Othello eventually sees her as *begrimed and black/ As mine own face* (Act 3, scene 3, lines 390–1). Newman associates maleness in the play with images of sight, and femaleness with images of hearing. Thus Othello says that Desdemona would *with a greedy ear/ Devour up my discourse* (Act 1, scene 3, lines 150–1). Newman sees this as female sexual desire being portrayed as an unsatisfied mouth. In her view Desdemona is punished by the male world for her desire, and especially for desiring a black man. Ironically, Othello is both the object of desire and the punisher, upholding white male values despite being black. Although Othello fulfils the Elizabethan racial stereotype of the black man (by being credulous, sensual and violent), Shakespeare does challenge race values by having a noble black hero and sympathetically potraying Desdemona's love for him. He challenges gender values by portraying Desdemona as both virtuous and desiring.

A number of critics, including Honigmann, have commented on the radical 'feminism' of Emilia's speech in Act 4, scene 3, in which she justifies female behaviour and claims a right to female desire. Honigmann also comments that Shakespeare challenges other stereotypes: the honest soldier (Iago); the slippery Florentine (Cassio); and the strumpet (Bianca).

PSYCHOANALYTICAL CRITICISM

As a drama of sexual jealousy, *Othello* lends itself to **psychoanalytical** interpretations (based on Freud's theory of repressed unconscious sexual urges). Iago is aware of the probable meaning of Cassio's 'dream' which he falsely reports as 'evidence' to Othello, but it says more about Iago's character than Cassio's. This report could hint at latent homosexuality in Iago. Some critics have pursued this possibility, suggesting that Iago resents losing Othello to Desdemona, or to Cassio. In one production in 1938 Olivier portrayed this interpretation, though he later admitted that it was not a great success.

Much has also been made of the symbolism of the strawberry-spotted handkerchief. Karen Newman calls it a 'snowballing **signifier**' – a symbol whose layers of meaning gradually accumulate. It begins as a love token given by Othello to Desdemona. In the Renaissance, strawberries symbolized virtue, but could also stand for false virtue, in the depiction of the strawberry plant with a snake hiding beneath it. It becomes a symbol of Desdemona's chastity. Its being *spotted* (as if with blood) stands first for the loss of her virginity, and then for loss of her reputation. It could be significant that the handkerchief passes through the hands of six different characters, including all the women. Newman even suggests that it could be seen as a fetish object, standing for the female lack of a penis, and for the male perception of female sexuality – especially given the magic supposedly woven into it.

Test your knowledge and understanding

1 Which critic thinks the focus on a handkerchief is silly?
2 Which relatively modern critic tends to idealize Othello?
3 Which critic accuses Othello of self-dramatizing and self-delusion?
4 Which critic finds that Othello has two styles of speech – beautiful and ugly?
5 Which critic links gender and race issues in the play?
6 Which famous actor portrayed Iago as homosexual?

Look back for the answers, then take a break.

HOW TO GET AN 'A' IN ENGLISH LITERATURE

In all your study, in coursework, and in exams, be aware of the following:

- **Characterization** – the characters and how we know about them (e.g. speech, actions, author description), their relationships, and how they develop.
- **Plot and structure** – story and how it is organized into parts or episodes.
- **Setting and atmosphere** – the changing physical scene and how it reflects the story (e.g. a storm reflecting chaos).
- **Style and language** – the author's choice of words, and literary devices such as imagery, and how these reflect the **mood**.
- **Viewpoint** – how the story is told (e.g. through an imaginary narrator, or in the third person but through the eyes of one character – 'She was furious – how dare he!').
- **Social and historical context** – the author's influences (see 'Context').
- **Critical approaches** – different ways in which the text has been, or could be, interpreted.

Develop your ability to:

- Relate **detail** to **broader content, meaning and style**.
- Show understanding of the author's **intentions, technique and meaning** (brief and appropriate comparisons with other works by the same author will gain marks).
- Give **personal response and interpretation**, backed up by **examples** and short **quotations**.
- **Evaluate** the author's achievement (how far does he/she succeed – give reasons).

Make sure you:

- Use **paragraphs** and **sentences** correctly.
- Write in an appropriate **register** – formal but not stilted.
- Use short, appropriate quotations as **evidence** of your understanding.
- Use **literary terms** correctly to explain how an author achieves effects.

THE EXAM ESSAY

PLANNING

You will probably have about 45 minutes for one essay. It is worth spending 5–10 minutes planning it. An excellent way to do this is in the three stages below.

1 **Brainstorm** your ideas, without worrying about their order yet.
2 **Arrange** the relevant ideas (the ones that really relate to the question) by numbering them in the order in which you will write the essay.
3 **Gather** your evidence and short quotes.

You could remember this as the **BAG** technique.

WRITING AND CHECKING

Then write the essay, allowing five minutes at the end for checking relevance, spelling, grammar and punctuation.

REMEMBER!

Stick to the question and always **back up** your points with evidence in the form of examples and short quotations. Note: you can use '…' for unimportant words missed out in a quotation.

MODEL ANSWERS

The next chapter consists of answers to two exam questions. Don't be put off if you think you couldn't write essays like this yet. You'll develop your skills if you work at them. Even if you're reading this the night before the exam, you can easily memorize the BAG technique in order to do your personal best.

The model answers are good examples to follow, but don't learn them by heart. It's better to pay close attention to the wording of the question and then allow yourself to think creatively.

Before reading the answers, you might like to do plans of your own to compare with the examples. The first model answer is given numbered points, with comments at the end, to show why it's a good answer. Work out for yourself what is good about the second answer (textual analysis).

MODEL ANSWERS

Question 1

Othello **is a man's play about men in a man's world: the female characters are only of secondary importance. Discuss.**

PLAN

- Social and historical context.
- Main focus is on men, and Othello's transformation.
- Plot male-driven.
- Male imagery.
- Dramatic role of women.
- Male attitudes to women in the play.
- Strength of female characters.
- Handkerchief as female symbol.

ESSAY

Shakespeare's England was a man's world. Unmarried women were expected to obey their fathers, married women their husbands. Married women could not own property, and were to a large extent regarded as their husbands' property themselves. This situation is reflected in the play, in that Brabantio is outraged that Desdemona has instead eloped with someone he would never have chosen. He complains: 'what's to become of my despised time/ Is nought but bitterness' (Act 1, scene 1), because he will now suffer loss of face. This is his first concern, not Desdemona's happiness. He calls Othello 'foul thief' because Othello has stolen his property. When Desdemona is summoned (Act 1, scene 3), she acknowledges, as a good wife, that she now owes more obedience to Othello.[1]

The play also reflects male domination in the sense that its male characters have more lines than its female ones, and it is called Othello's tragedy, not Desdemona's. This male focus was not automatic, as can be seen from 'Romeo and Juliet',[2] but there is one practical reason for it: in Shakespeare's time the female characters were played by boy actors.[3] However, this is only a partial explanation. Shakespeare seems to have been largely concerned with the transformation of his hero. At first Othello is the noble character who has the quiet command and self-confidence to calm his accusers in Act 1, scene 2, with the lines 'Keep up your bright swords, for the dew will rust them.' Worked on by Iago, he gradually breaks down and eventually has a fit. His disjointed language shows his disintegrating character: 'Pish! Noses, ears and lips. Is't possible? Confess! handkerchief! O devil!' (Act 4, scene 1). Desdemona goes through no similar process of transformation, merely moving from confident happiness to puzzled distress. This probably means that Shakespeare was less interested in her, although the critic A.J. Honigmann argues that it shows her greater constancy.[4]

The plot itself is at first driven by the demands of the male world. The move to Cyprus is required because of a threat of war. Desdemona goes there only because Othello is sent there by the all-male Venetian senate. The scheming of which Desdemona is an innocent victim is about male concerns: Iago's hatred of Othello, first revealed to us when Iago reassures Roderigo, and his resentment of Cassio, whom he sneeringly dismisses as 'a great arithmetician', ignorant of real war (Act 1, scene 1). The scene in which Iago launches his campaign of corruption is set entirely in the male world – a drunken brawl between soldiers meant to be guarding the city (Act 2, scene 3).[5]

The maleness of the play as a whole is also seen in its imagery. The most obvious examples are those relating to maritime life, as in Othello's metaphorical 'very sea-mark of my utmost sail' (Act 5, scene 2) and to entrapment and imprisonment, as in Iago's reference to 'the net/ That shall enmesh them all' (Act 2, scene 3). However, the play's sexual animal imagery, such as Iago's provocative suggestion to Brabantio that 'an old black ram/ Is tupping your white ewe!' (Act 1, scene 1), could also be seen as male rather than female, at least in Shakespeare's world.[6]

Although women are marginalized in the world of the play, they are important dramatically. Othello's military man's world is contrasted with Desdemona's domestic world when she insists that she seeks Cassio's reinstatement only for Othello's own good, as if asking him to wear gloves, or eat nourishing food (Act 3, scene 3). When she asks when he will speak to Cassio, she suggests mealtimes: 'tonight at supper', 'Tomorrow dinner'. Desdemona is also vital to the plot as it is Othello's love for her that makes him vulnerable. Similarly, Cassio is made vulnerable to Iago's scheming by his affair with Bianca – Iago gets him to discuss her while Othello spies and thinks the discussion is about Desdemona (Act 4, scene 1). It is Emilia who enables Iago's use of the handkerchief as 'evidence', yet it is also Emilia who bravely exposes his treachery.[7]

Male attitudes to women are crucial to the play. Othello at first adores Desdemona, as shown when he arrives in Cyprus (Act 2, scene 1). She is his 'soul's joy', his happiness is 'too much joy' and makes him 'prattle out of fashion'. Cassio almost worships Desdemona, as if she were a goddess to whom the very forces of nature '... having sense of beauty, do omit/ Their mortal natures' – allowing her safe passage (Act 2, scene 1). Iago has no such respect for women or for Emilia. When she says she has something for him, he says 'You have a thing for me? it is a common thing'. His failure to respect or understand her means that it never occurs to him that she will expose him.[8]

Though given fewer lines than the men, the three female characters are strong in their ways. Desdemona is assertive enough to defy her father and elope with a Moor. She also shows assertiveness when she insists on going to Cyprus with Othello, whereas a wife would normally stay at home. Some critics say that she is too passive at the end, dutifully allowing her own murder, but this has to be seen in the context of her still being in shock at being accused. Bianca breaks the mould of the 'strumpet' by being devoted to Cassio – she counts the hours since she saw him last (Act 3, scene 4) – and by her distress when he is attacked (Act 5, scene 1). We see Emilia's commitment to justice in her wish that villains should be whipped round the world (Act 4, scene 2), and in her strongly 'feminist' speech asserting women's right to have needs and desires (Act 4, scene 3). We see her love for Desdemona in her fierce defence of her to Othello and her exposure of Iago.[9]

Finally, it is striking that the most powerful symbol in the play – the handkerchief – is feminine. It was made by a prophetess, given by an Egyptian woman to Othello's mother, who gave it to him, and it now belongs to Desdemona. Since it is said to have magical power, and is the most important means by which Iago convinces Othello of Desdemona's guilt, it assumes huge dramatic significance. This seems to provide an appropriate symbol for the role of women in the play. Although they do not actively progress the plot as often as the male characters, they are of equal dramatic significance, as well as showing a different kind of strength within the confines of gender roles in Shakespeare's world.[10]

WHAT EARNED THE MARKS?

1 Shows how the play reflects its social and historical context.
2 Awareness of literary context.
3 Awareness of the play as theatre, with what that implies practically.
4 Awareness of alternative critical approaches.
5 Understanding of the plot and the world it creates.
6 Appreciation of language and ability to discuss it with appropriate terminology.
7 Understanding of characters having dramatic roles.
8 Understanding of male attitudes; good character analysis on Iago.
9 Good character analysis.
10 Understanding of symbolism, leading neatly to brief conclusion.

Question 2: textual analysis

Some exam boards require you to comment on a passage from the play, reproduced in the exam paper. Your teacher will know whether your board does this. Even if it does not, the following example will be useful, as all your essays should be based on textual evidence.

If commenting on a passage, you should focus closely on its language, while showing that you are aware of its context within the play as a whole. You should stick to the question and make use of any hints given.

MODEL ANSWERS

Read *Othello*, Act 3, scene 3, from Othello's line *Give me a living reason she's disloyal* (line 412 in the Arden edition) to the end of the scene. Comment on how and why Othello's attitude towards Desdemona and Cassio develops and how this is shown.

You could consider, together with your own ideas:

◆ Iago's technique and how Othello's language shows his response to it.
◆ The effect of imagery.
◆ Othello's relationship and how it develops during the passage.

ESSAY

At this point in the scene, Iago has been working Othello to a fever pitch of jealous doubt, but Othello has not yet given in entirely. He still requires proof, a 'living reason she's disloyal', before he will accept Desdemona's infidelity as a fact. Iago realizes that Othello is now jealous enough to believe an unsubstantiated account of a dream as 'proof', and that Othello now almost wants to hear this 'proof' rather than remain in the agony of uncertainty. Hence he launches into his account of Cassio's 'dream', feigning reluctance as he has done before. Indeed he can now make a more genuine claim to reluctance, since earlier Othello has physically attacked him. This is why Iago now says that he is spurred on 'by foolish honesty and love'.

We assume that two soldiers might sleep next to each other, perhaps after a night's drinking. Iago also gives a plausible reason for his being awake, and an explanation for Cassio's sleep-talking which has the advantage of showing Cassio in a bad light – he is 'loose of soul'. Iago's account of Cassio's endearments to the imagined Desdemona, and of Cassio gripping his hand, kissing him and laying his leg on Iago's thigh, are calculated to incense Othello by making him imagine what Cassio would do with Desdemona. He is so caught up in this picture that he does not think it strange that Iago apparently lay quietly putting up with Cassio's behaviour.

Iago uses another favourite technique when he seems to defend Cassio and deny the strength of this 'proof': 'Nay, this was but a dream.' However, he admits that it may 'help to

101

thicken other proofs'. The effect on Othello is shown by his outburst, 'I'll tear her all to pieces!' The line shows how Othello has changed from the noble commander and adoring husband. This proof of Othello's growing conviction encourages Iago to produce further 'evidence', in the shape of the handkerchief. A skilled trickster, he strengthens his case by disclaiming any special knowledge of the handkerchief's significance ('I know not that ...'), and presents Othello with an insulting and inflaming picture of Cassio wiping his beard with it.

We see how much this affects Othello's feelings for Cassio by his wish to kill him forty thousand times over. The line 'Now do I see 'tis true' shows that Othello is finally convinced, so that he makes a ritual of blowing his foolish love to heaven. Now we see how far he has been corrupted by Iago: he summons 'black vengeance' from hell in preparation for killing Desdemona, and replaces all his love with hate. The image of 'aspics' tongues' gives us a sense of the poisonous, murderous and bestial urges that Othello now feels, as does, in a more earthy way, the repetition 'O blood, blood, blood!'

Iago's pretended attempt to calm Othello reinforces his credibility while actually stirring Othello up even more. His extended simile comparing his murderous determination to the one-way tide of the Pontic Sea is terrifying in its icy power. It also hints at the self-dramatizing tendency that some critics (such as Leavis and Wilson Knight) have seen in Othello's speeches. He is comparing himself to a mighty ocean.

The vow which Othello grandly makes 'by yond marble heaven' both suggests a coldness of purpose which will enable him to steel his passion to effective action, and shows his fixed determination now that he is finally convinced. Iago's kneeling beside him to make his own vow is a master-stroke of dramatic ingenuity, calculated to make Othello see Iago as the one man truly on his side. Iago heightens the effect by imitating Othello's grandiose appeal to cosmic forces.

We now see that whereas earlier in the scene Othello was prepared to attack Iago, now he is grateful to him, and confident that Iago will kill Cassio. Perhaps sensing that Othello is forgetting Desdemona, Iago reminds Othello of her with the line 'But let her live.' This may also be a deliberate prompt to Othello to do the opposite – and plan her death. Certainly this is its effect: Othello curses her and declares his intention to kill her. His oxymoron, 'the fair devil' shows that he thinks he has seen through her at last.

The most significant development in Othello's relationship with Iago is shown right at the end of the scene. Othello promotes Iago to the position formerly held by Cassio, and Iago, false to the last, confirms his loyalty to Othello.

Taking It Further

Books

(including those referred to in the guide)

Bradley, A.C., *Shakespearean Tragedy* (Macmillan, 1992)

Honigmann, E.A.J., *Othello* (Arden Shakespeare, 2001). Very comprehensive introduction and textual notes.

Kermode, Frank, *Shakespeare's Language* (Penguin, 2000)

Muir, Kenneth, *Othello* (Penguin New Shakespeare, 1996). Good introduction.

Wain, John (ed.), *Shakespeare's Othello* (Palgrave Casebook Series, 1994). Includes extracts from Rymer, Johnson, Coleridge, Bradley, Eliot, Wilson Knight, Leavis, Norris and Newman.

Websites

www.bbc.co.uk/education/asguru/english/08shakespeare/index.shtml Very useful site including exam objectives and a sample essay on *Othello* with detailed commentary.

www.shakespeare.org.uk/main/1 Background to texts, Shakespeare at school, FAQs. Click link to 'Study Materials' for 'Othello: Race, Place and Identity', which includes a section on the play in performance (with images of famous Othellos).

http://web.singnet.com.sg/~yisheng/notes/shakespeare/othello_b.htm Gives much of A.C. Bradley's 1904 essays.

www.allshakespeare.com/plays/othello Searchable Shakespeare texts, essays, key quotes, etc. Some sections require a pass, obtainable for a one-off small fee.

www.dmax.com/Shakespeare Complete Works of Shakespeare

www.rdg.ac.uk./globe/home.htm Information on Shakespeare's Globe and other contemporary theatres, and on the modern Globe.

http://special.lib.gla.ac.uk/exhibns/month/july2001.html
Interesting and well-illustrated feature on the First Folio edition of Shakespeare's plays (1623).

Films

There are several screen adaptations of *Othello* available on video and DVD. One of the best modern ones is *Castle Rock* (1995), starring Laurence Fishburne (Othello) and Kenneth Branagh (Iago), directed by Oliver Parker. Branagh plays Iago sympathetically. Michael Maloney plays Roderigo almost as a madman.

GLOSSARY OF LITERARY TERMS

alliteration the repetition, for poetic effect, of consonant sounds.

atmosphere the emotional feeling generated, especially by the setting and how it is described, preparing us for the action.

blank verse unrhymed **iambic pentameter**.

domestic tragedy a tragedy set at least partly in and around the home and focusing on love and marriage rather than war or politics.

dramatic irony when the audience knows an important fact of which at least one character on stage is ignorant.

genre literary form.

hendiadys poetic device in which two related words are used, joined by 'and'. They can either replace a single word, as in *play and trifle with your reverence*, or an adjective and a noun, as in *as loving his own pride and purposes*.

iambic pentameter verse in which each line consists of five pairs (*iams*) of syllables, each pair containing an unstressed syllable followed by a stressed one.

image word picture bringing an idea to life by appealing to the senses.

imagery the use of **images**.

irony the use of a statement to suggest its opposite; see also **dramatic irony**.

metaphor an **image** speaking of something as if it were something else.

mood the emotional effect of the play's action and of the feelings expressed by its characters.

mystery plays religious plays enacting the Christ story, with set characters not intended to be realistic.

prose text not in verse.

psychoanalytical relating to Freud's theory of repressed unconscious sexual urges.

GLOSSARY

resolution the way in which the play reaches a satisfying ending, allowing the audience to go away with a sense of calm fulfilment.

revenge tragedy popular dramatic **genre** characterized by secret plotting and trickery, and by one or more violent revenge murders occurring at the end of the play.

signifier a concrete symbol standing for a concept.

simile an **image** using 'like' or 'as', comparing one thing with another.

soliloquy speech made by one character alone on stage.

stereotype fixed expectation of one section of society.

subplot subsidiary plot coinciding with the main plot and often reflecting aspects of it.

tragedy play featuring a noble hero who eventually dies through a fatal weakness, coupled with fate.

Index

alliteration 63
Aphrodite 6

Bianca 18, **19–20**, 26, 29, 66
Brabantio **20–1**
Bradley, A.C. 89–90, 91

Cassio **18**, 26, 29, 35
Cinthio 1–2
Clown **22**
Coleridge, Samuel Taylor 88–9
Cyprus 6

dating of play 6, 39
Desdemona **17**, 25–6, 35, 53
Duke of Venice **21**

Eliot, T.S. 90
Emilia **18–19**, 26, 79–80

feminist criticism 92–3
French, Marilyn 92–3

gender 97–100
genre 2
Gratiano **21**

Hamlet 4, 89
Holland, Philemon 2
Honigmann, A.J. 27, 42, 73, 93
honour 33, 56

Iago **13–16**
  deception 30, 35–6, 38, 41, 57, 101–3
  motives 4, 13–15, 27–8, 51, 54, 61, 90
  sexuality 24–5, 26, 93–4
  stage villain 15–16, 30, 44
imagery 24, 36–8, 45, 50, 62, 64

Johnson, Samuel 88

Knight, G. Wilson 92

Leavis, F.R. 90–1
Leo, John 2, 4
Lewkenor 2
Lodovico **21**

Macbeth 10, 37, 40, 41, 64
Montano **21**
Moors 4
Muir, Kenneth 92

Newman, Karen 93, 94
Norris, Christopher 91–2

Othello **10–13**
  inconsistent 12, 91
  jealousy 28–9, 30–1, 101–3
  language 34–5, 37–8, 47, 62, 68, 92
  lover 25, 50, 54
  man of action 10, 56, 89

noble 11
vulnerable 11

Pliny 2
Pory, John 2
Prometheus 77
prose 34
psychoanalytical criticism 93–4

reputation *see* honour
rhetoric 34
rhyme 49
Roderigo **20**
Rymer, Thomas 88

Seneca 39
settings 30, 41, 44

soliloquies 30, 41
STAR formula 39–40
story 7–9
structure 39–43

themes, overlapping 23
  appearances 29–31
  individual, society and 32–3, 46
  jealousy 27–9
  love and sex 24–7
  race 4, 31–2, 47
  women 23–4
timescale 42–3
tragedy 2

Venice 4–6
verse, blank 34

NOTES

NOTES

NOTES

NOTES

NOTES

NOTES

NOTES

NOTES